The Princess Pocahontas

Virginia Watson

Alpha Editions

This edition published in 2024

ISBN 9789362097545

Design and Setting By
Alpha Editions
www.alphaedis.com
Email - info@alphaedis.com

Contents

THE WHITE FIGURE MOVED RAPIDLY

INTRODUCTION

To most of us who have read of the early history of Virginia only in our school histories, Pocahontas is merely a figure in one dramatic scene—her rescue of John Smith. We see her in one mental picture only, kneeling beside the prostrate Englishman, her uplifted hands warding off the descending tomahawk.

By chance I began to read more about the settlement of the English at Jamestown and Pocahontas' connection with it, and the more I read the more interesting and real she grew to me. The old chronicles gave me the facts, and guided by these, my imagination began to follow the Indian maiden as she went about the forests or through the villages of the Powhatans.

We are growing up in this new country of ours. And just as when children get older they begin to feel curious about the childhood of their own parents, so we have gained a new curiosity about the early history of our country. The earlier histories and stories dealing with the Indians and the wars between them and the colonists made the red man a devil incarnate, with no redeeming virtue but that of courage. Now, however, there is a new spirit of understanding. We are finding out how often it was the Indian who was wronged and the white man who wronged him. Many records there are of treaties faithfully kept by the Indians and faithlessly broken by the colonists. Virginia was the first permanent English settlement on this continent, and if not the *most* important, at least equally as important to our future development as that of New England. From how small a seed, sown on that island of Jamestown in 1607, has sprung the mighty State, that herself has scattered seeds of other states and famous men and women to multiply and enrich America. And amid what dangers did this seed take root! But for one girl's aid—as far as man may judge—it would have been uprooted and destroyed.

In truth, when I look over the whole world history, I can find no other child of thirteen, boy or girl, who wielded such a far-reaching influence over the future of a nation. But for the protection and aid which Pocahontas coaxed from Powhatan for her English friends at Jamestown, the Colony would have perished from starvation or by the arrows of the hostile Indians. And the importance of this Colony to the future United States was so great that we owe to Pocahontas somewhat the same gratitude, though in a lesser degree, that France owes to her Joan of Arc.

Pocahontas's greatest service to the colonists lay not in the saving of Captain Smith's life, but in her continued succour to the starving settlement. Indeed, there are historians who have claimed that the story of her rescue of Smith is an invention without foundation. But in opposition to this view let me quote from "The American Nation: A History." Lyon Gardiner Tyler, author of the volume "England in America" says:

"The credibility of this story has been attacked.... Smith was often inaccurate and prejudiced in his statements, but that is far from saying that he deliberately mistook plain objects of sense or concocted a story having no foundation."

and from "The New International Encyclopaedia":

"Until Charles Deane attacked it (the story of Pocahontas's rescue of Smith) in 1859, it was seldom questioned, but, owing largely to his criticisms, it soon became generally discredited. In recent years, however, there has been a tendency to retain it."

It is in Smith's own writings, "General Historie of Virginia" and "A True Relation," that we find the best and fullest accounts of these first days at Jamestown. He tells us not only what happened, but how the new country looked; what kinds of game abounded; how the Indians lived, and what his impressions of their customs were. Smith was ignorant of certain facts about the Indians with which we are now familiar. The curious ceremony which took place in the hut in the forest, just before Powhatan freed Smith and allowed him to return to Jamestown, was one he could not comprehend. Modern historians believe that it was probably the ceremony of adoption by which Smith was made one of the tribe.

In many places in this story I have not only followed closely Smith's own narrative of what occurred, but have made use of the very words in which he recorded the conversations. For instance the incident related on page 101 was set down by Smith himself; on pages 144, 154, 262 the words are those of Smith as given in his history; on pages 173, 195, 260, 300 the words of Powhatan or Pocahontas as Smith relates them.

There may be readers of this story who will want to know what became of Pocahontas. She fell ill of a fever just as she was about to sail home for Virginia and died in Gravesend, where she was buried. Her son Thomas Rolfe was educated in England and went to Virginia when he was grown. His daughter Jane married John Bolling, and among their descendants have been many famous men and women, including Edith Bolling (Mrs. Galt) who married President Woodrow Wilson.

CHAPTER I

THE RETURN OF THE WARRIORS

Through the white forest came Opechanchanough and his braves, treading as silently as the flakes that fell about them. From their girdles hung fresh scalp locks which their silent Monachan owners did not miss.

But Opechanchanough, on his way to Werowocomoco to tell The Powhatan of the victory he had won over his enemies, did not feel quite sure that he had slain all the war party against which he and his Pamunkey braves had gone forth. The unexpected snow, coming late in the winter, had been blown into their eyes by the wind so that they could not tell whether some of the Monachans had not succeeded in escaping their vengeance. Perhaps, even yet, so near to the wigwams of his brother's town, the enemy might have laid an ambush. Therefore, it behooved them to be on their guard, to look behind each tree for crouching figures and to harken with all their ears that not even a famished squirrel might crack a nut unless they could point out the bough on which it perched.

Opechanchanough led the long thin line that threaded its way through the broad cutting between huge oaks, still bronze with last year's leaves. He held his head high and to himself he framed the words of the song of triumph he meant to sing to The Powhatan, as the chief of the Powhatans was called. Then, suddenly before his face shot an arrow.

At a shout from their leader, the long line swung itself to the right, and fifty arrows flew to the northward, the direction from which danger might be expected. Still there was silence, no outcry from an ambushed enemy, no sign of other human creatures.

Opechanchanough consulted with his braves whence had the arrow come; and even while they talked, another arrow from the right whizzed before his face.

"A bad archer," he grunted, "who cannot hit me with two shots." Then pointing to a huge oak that forked half way up, he commanded:

"Bring him to me."

Two braves rushed forward to the tree, on which all eyes were now fixed. It was difficult to distinguish anything through the falling snow and the mass of its flakes that had gathered in the crotch. All was white there, yet there was something white which moved, and the two braves on reaching the tree trunk yelled in delight and disdain.

The white figure moved rapidly now. Swinging itself out on a branch and catching hold of a higher one, it seemed determined to retreat from its pursuers to the very summit of the tree. But the braves did not waste time in climbing after it; they leapt up in the air like panthers, caught the branch and swung it vigorously back and forth so that the creature's feet slipped from under it and it fell into their outstretched arms.

Not waiting even to investigate the white bundle of fur, the warriors, surrounded by their curious fellows, bore it to Opechanchanough, and laid it on the ground before him. He knelt and lifted up the cap of rabbit skin with flapping ears that hid the face, then cried out in angry astonishment:

"Pocahontas! What meaneth this trick?"

And the white fur bundle, rising to her feet, laughed and laughed till the oldest and staidest warrior could not help smiling. But Opechanchanough did not smile; he was too angry. His dignity suffered at thus being made the sport of a child. He shook his niece, saying:

"What meaneth this, I ask? What meaneth this?"

Pocahontas then ceased laughing and answered:

"I wanted to see for myself how brave thou wert. Uncle, and to know just how great warriors such as ye are act when an enemy is upon them. I am not so bad an archer, Uncle; I would not shoot thee, so I aimed beyond thee. But it was such fun to sit up there in the tree and watch all of you halt so suddenly."

Her explanation set most of the party laughing again.

"In truth, is she well named," they cried—"Pocahontas, Little Wanton."

"I have yet another name," she said to an old brave who stood nearest her. "Knowest thou it not?—Matoaka, Little Snow Feather. Always when the moons of popanow (winter) bring us snow it calls me out to play. 'Come, Snow Feather,' it cries, 'come out and run with me and toss me up into the air.'"

Her uncle had now recovered his calm and was about to start forward again. Turning to the two who had captured Pocahontas, he commanded:

"Since we have taken a prisoner we will bear her to Powhatan for judgment and safekeeping. Had we shot back into the tree she might have been killed. See that she doth not escape you."

Then he stalked ahead through the forest, paying no further attention to Pocahontas.

The young braves looked sheepishly at each other and at their captive, not at all relishing their duty. Opechanchanough was not to be disobeyed, yet it was no easy thing to hold a young maid against her will, and no force or even show of force might be used against a daughter of the mighty werowance (chieftain).

Seeing their uncertainty, Pocahontas started to run to the left and they to pursue her. They came up with her before she had gone as far as three bows' lengths and led her back gently to their place in the line. Then she walked sedately along as if unconscious of their presence, until they were off their guard, believing she had resigned herself to the situation, when she sprang off to the right and was again captured and led back. She knew that they dared not bind her, and she took advantage of this to lead them in truth a dance, first to one side and then to the other. Behind them their comrades jeered and laughed each time the maiden ran away.

The regular order of the warpath was now no longer preserved. They had advanced to a point where there was no longer any possibility of danger from hostile attack. Werowocomoco lay now but a short distance away; already the smoke from its lodges could be seen across the cleared fields that surrounded the village of Powhatan. The older warriors were walking in groups, talking over their deeds of valor performed that day, and praising those of several of the young braves who had fought for the first time. Pocahontas and her captors had now fallen further behind.

Though well satisfied with the results of her enterprise and amusement, Pocahontas had no mind to be brought into her home as a captive, even though it be half in jest. Her father might not consider it so amusing and, moreover, she did not like to be outwitted. She was so busy thinking that she forgot to continue her game and walked quietly ahead, keeping up with the longer strides of the warriors by occasional little runs forward. The braves, their own heads full of their first campaign, kept fingering lovingly the scalps at their girdles, and paid little attention to her.

She stooped as if to fasten her moccasin, then, as their impetus carried them a few feet ahead of her before they stopped for her to come up, she darted like a flash to the left and had slid down into a little hollow before they thought of starting after her.

It was now almost dark and her white fur was indistinguishable against the snow below. Before they had reached the bottom, Pocahontas, who knew every inch of the ground that was less familiar to men from her uncle's village, had slipped back into the forest which skirted the fields the pursuers were now speeding across, and was lost at once in the darkness.

Opechanchanough knew nothing of this escape. He meant to explain to his royal brother how much mischief a child might do who was not kept at home performing squaw duties in her wigwam. And Powhatan's favorite daughter or not, Pocahontas should be kept waiting outside her father's lodge until he had related his important business and had recounted all the glorious deeds done by his Pamunkeys.

Now they had come to Werowocomoco itself, and the noise of their shoutings and of their war drums brought the inhabitants running out of their wigwams. As the Pamunkeys were an allied tribe, their cause against a common enemy was the same, yet the rejoicings at the victory against the Monachans was somewhat less than it would have been had the conquerors been Powhatans themselves. However, Opechanchanough and his braves could not complain of their reception, and runners sped ahead to advise Powhatan of their coming, while all the population of their village crowded about them, the men questioning, the boys fingering the scalps and each boasting how many he would have at his girdle when he was grown.

The great Werowance was not in his ceremonial lodge but in the one in which he ordinarily slept and ate when at Werowocomoco. Opechanchanough paused at the opening of the lodge and ordered:

"When I call out then bring ye in Pocahontas, and we shall see what Powhatan thinks of a squaw child that shoots at warriors."

The lodge was almost dark when he entered it. Before the fire in the centre he could see his brother Powhatan seated, and on each side of him one of his wives. Then he made out the features of his nephew Nautauquas and Pocahontas' younger sister, Cleopatra (for so it was the English later understood the girl's strange Indian name). They had evidently just been eating supper and the dogs behind them were gnawing the wild turkey bones that had been thrown to them. At Powhatan's feet crouched a child in a dark robe, with face in the shadow.

Powhatan greeted his brother gravely and bade him be seated. The lodge soon filled with braves packed closely together, and about the opening crowded all who could, and these repeated to the men and squaws left outside the words that were spoken within.

Proudly Opechanchanough began to tell how he had tracked the Monachans to a hill above the river, and how he and his war party had fallen upon them, driving them down the steep banks, slaying and scalping, even swimming into the icy water to seize those who sought to escape. And The Powhatan nodded in approval, uttering now and again a word of praise. When Opechanchanough had finished his recital the shaman, or medicine-man, rose and sang a song of praise about the brave Pamunkeys, brothers of the Powhatans.

Then, one after another, Opechanchanough's braves told of their personal exploits.

"I," sang one, "I, the Forest Wolf, have devoured mine enemy. Many suns shall set red between the forest trees, but none so red as the blood that flowed when my sharp knife severed his scalp lock."

And as each recited his deeds his words were received with clappings of hands and grunts of approval.

Powhatan gave orders to open the guest lodge and to prepare a feast for the victors. Then Opechanchanough rose again to speak. After he had finished another song of triumph, he turned to Powhatan and asked:

"Brother, how long hath it been that thy warriors keep within their lodges, leaving to young squaws the duty of sentinels who cannot distinguish friends from foes?"

Powhatan gazed at the speaker in astonishment.

"What dost thou mean by such strange words?" asked the chief.

"As we returned through the forest," explained Opechanchanough, "before we reached the boundary of thy fields, while we still believed that a part of the Monachans might lie in ambush for us there, an arrow, shot from the westward, flew before my face. Then came a second arrow out of the branches of an oak tree. We took the bowman prisoner, and what thinkest thou we found?—a squaw child!"

"A squaw child!" repeated Powhatan in astonishment. "Was it one of this village?"

"Even so. Brother. I have her captive outside that thou mayst pronounce judgment upon one who endangers thus the life of thy brother and who forgetteth she is not a boy. Bring in the prisoner," he commanded.

But no one came forward. The young braves to whom Pocahontas had been entrusted kept wisely on the outskirts of the crowd.

Then the little sombre figure at Powhatan's feet rose and stood with the firelight shining on her face and dark hair and asked in a gentle voice:

"Didst thou want me, mine uncle?"

"Pocahontas," exclaimed Opechanchanough, "how camest thou here ahead of us, and in that dark robe?"

"Pocahontas can run even better than she can shoot. Uncle, and the changing of a robe is the matter but of a moment."

"What meaneth this, Matoaka?" asked Powhatan, making use of her special intimate name, which signified Little Snow Feather. He spoke in a low tone, but one so stern that Cleopatra shivered and rejoiced that she was not the culprit.

"It was but a joke, my father," answered Pocahontas. "I meant no harm." She hung her head and waited until he should speak again.

"I will have no such jokes in my land," he said angrily, "remember that."

With a gesture of his hand and a whispered word of command he sent the Pamunkey braves to the guest lodge. Opechanchanough, still angry at the ridicule that a child had brought upon him, lingered to ask;

"Wilt thou not punish her?"

"Surely I will," Powhatan answered. "Go ye all to the guest lodge and I will follow. Away, Nautauquas, and carry my pipe thither."

They were now alone in the lodge, the great chief over thirty tribes and his daughter, who still stood with downcast head. The Powhatan gazed at her curiously. She waited for him to speak, then as he kept silent, she turned and looked straight into his face and asked:

"Father, dost thou know how hard it is to be a girl? Nautauquas, my brother, is a swift runner, yet I am fleeter than he. I can shoot as straight as he, though not so far. I can go without food and drink as long as he. I can dance without fatigue when he is panting. Yet Nautauquas is to be a great brave and I—thou bidst remember to be a squaw. Is it not hard, my father? Why then didst thou give me strong arms and legs and a spirit that will not be still? Do not blame me. Father, because I must laugh and run and play."

As she spoke she slipped to her knees and embraced his feet and when she had ceased speaking, she smiled up fearless into his face.

Powhatan tried not to be moved by the child's pleading. Yet he was a chief who always harkened to the excuses made by offenders brought before him and judged them justly, if sometimes harshly. This child of his was as dear to him as a running stream to summer heat. If at times its spray dashed too high, could he be angry?

And Pocahontas, seeing that his anger had gone from him, stood up and laid her head against his arm. She did not have to be told that the mighty Powhatan loved no wife nor child of his as he loved her. Then his hand stroked her soft hair and cheek, and she knew that she was forgiven.

"Thine uncle is very angry," he said.

"If thou couldst but have seen him. Father, when the arrow whizzed," and she laughed gaily in memory of the picture.

"I have promised to punish thee."

"Yea, as thou wilt." But she did not speak as if afraid.

"Hear what I charge thee," he said in mock solemnity. "Thou shalt embroider for me with thine own hands—thou that carest not for squaw's needles—a robe of raccoon skin in quills and bits of precious shells."

Pocahontas laughed.

"That is no punishment. 'Tis a strange thing, but when I do things I like not for those I love, why, then I pleasure in doing them. I will fashion for thee such a robe as thou hast never seen. Oh! I know how beautiful it will be. I will make new patterns such as no squaw hath ever dreamed of before. But thou wilt never be really angry with me. Father, wilt thou?" she questioned pleadingly. "And if I should at any time do what displeaseth thee, and thou wearest this robe I make thee, then let it be a token between us and when I touch it thou wilt forgive me and grant what I ask of thee?"

And Powhatan promised and smiled on her before he set forth for the guest lodge.

CHAPTER II

POCAHONTAS AND THE MEDICINE MAN

Some months later on there came a hot day such as sometimes appears in the early spring. The sun shone with almost as much power as if the corn were high above the ground in which it had only just been planted with song and the observance of ancient sacred rites and dances. Little leaves glistened like fish scales, as they gently unfurled themselves on the walnut and persimmon trees about Werowocomoco, and in the forest the ground was covered with flowers. The children tied them together and tossed them as balls to and fro or wound them into chaplets for their hair; the old squaws searched among them for certain roots and leaves for dyes to stain the grass cloth they spun, called pemmenaw.

The boys played hunters, pretending their dogs were wild beasts, but the bears and wolves did not always understand the parts assigned them and frolicked and leaped up in delight upon their little masters instead of turning upon them ferociously. The elder braves lay before their lodges, many of them idling in the sunshine, others busied themselves making arrows, fitting handles to stone knives or knotting crab nets. Two slaves, brought home prisoners by a war party, were hollowing out a dugout, which the Powhatans used instead of the birchbark canoes preferred by other tribes. They had cut down an oak tree that, judging from its rings, must have been an acorn when Powhatan was a papoose, seventy years before. They had burned out a portion of the outer and inner bark and were now hacking at the heart of the wood with sharp obsidian axes.

The squaws were also all busy out of doors, though they chatted in groups as eagerly as if their energy were being expended by their tongues only. Many were at work scraping deerskin to soften it before they cut it into robes for themselves or into moccasins for the men. Here and there little puffs of smoke that seemed to come from beneath the earth testified to the dinners that were being cooked under heated stones.

Pocahontas was seated upon a small hill overlooking the village. As the chief's daughter, it was only on special occasions and as an honored guest, that she joined the knots of squaws or maidens chatting before the wigwams. But she was not alone now in solitary grandeur. She was accustomed to surround herself, when she desired company, with a number of younger girls of the tribe who obeyed her, less because she was the daughter of the feared werowance, than because she had a way with her that made it pleasant to do as she willed and difficult to oppose her.

Cleopatra, her youngest sister, sat beside her, trying to coax a squirrel on the branch above them to come down and eat some parched corn from her hands.

Over Pocahontas's knees was spread a robe of raccoon skin, smooth, painted in a wide border. Along the edge of this she was embroidering a deep pattern of white beads made from sea shells. A basket of reeds beside her was full of other beads, large and small, white, red, yellow and blue.

"What doth thy pattern mean, Pocahontas?" asked the girl nearest her. "As it is not one any of our mothers hath ever wrought before, thou must have a meaning for it in thy mind." "Yes," assented the worker, "it differeth from all other patterns because my father differeth from all other werowances. It meaneth this that I sing:

"Powhatan is a mighty chief,As long as the river floweth,As long as the sky upholdeth,As long as the oak tree groweth,So long shall his name be known.

"See, this line is for the river, this one that goeth up straight is the oak tree and this long line all wavy is the heavens. I make this for my father because I am so proud of him."

"But why, Pocahontas," asked another of her companions, "dost thou not use more of these red beads? They are so like fire, like the blood of an enemy; why dost thou refer the white?"

Pocahontas held her bone needle still for a moment and her face wore a puzzled expression.

"I cannot answer thee exactly, Deer-Eye, since I do not know myself. I love the white beads as I love best to wear a white robe myself, or a white rabbit hood in winter. In the woods I always pick the white flowers, and I love the white wild pigeon best of all the birds except the white seagull. And the white soft clouds high in the heavens I love better than the red and yellow ones when the sun goeth down to sleep in the west. Yet I cannot say why it is so."

As noon approached the day grew hotter, and the fingers wearied of the work. Down in the village the men had ceased their activities and lay stretched out on the shady side of the lodges; only the squaws preparing dinner were still busy.

"Let us go to the waterfall," cried Pocahontas, jumping up suddenly. "Each of you go and beg some food from her mother and hurry back here. I will put my work away and await ye here."

The maidens flew down the hill while Pocahontas and Cleopatra carried the robe and the basket to their lodge. Then, a few minutes later, they were rejoined by their companions and all started off laughing as they ran through the woods.

The stream that flowed into the great river below was now still wide with its spring fulness. A mile away from Werowocomoco it fell over high rocks, then rushing down a gentle incline bubbled over smooth rocky slabs, and made a deep pool below them.

The maidens tossed off their skirts and stood for a moment hesitatingly on the shore. Mocking-birds sang in the oaks above them, startled by their shrill young voices, and on the bare branches of a sycamore tree that had been killed by a lightning bolt a score of raccoons lay curled up in the sunshine.

Pocahontas was the first to spring into the stream, but her comrades quickly followed her, laughing, pushing, crying out the first chill of the water. Only Cleopatra remained standing on the shore.

"Come," called Pocahontas to her; "why dost thou tarry, lazy one?"

"I will not come. The water is too cold."

Cleopatra was about to slip on her skirt again when her sister splashed through the stream to her and half pushed, half pulled her into the pool and then to the rocks partly submerged in the water. There was much screaming and calling, slipping from the rocks into the pool and clambering from the pool back on to the rocks. The water was now pleasantly warm and the dinner awaiting them was forgotten in the pleasure of the first bath of the season.

Deer-Eye, in trying to pull herself back on the rock, caught hold of Cleopatra's foot, who slipped on the mossy surface and fell backwards into the water, hitting her head against a sharp edge. She lost consciousness and sank down into the pool.

Almost before she had disappeared beneath the water Pocahontas had sprung after her, and groping about on the fine smooth sand of the bottom, she caught hold of her sister and brought her to the surface.

Then, with the aid of the terrified maidens, she lifted her up on the bank, the blood flowing freely from a cut on her head. After vainly trying to staunch the wound with damp moss, Pocahontas commanded:

"Hasten as though the Iroquois were coming, and cut me some strong branches."

They obeyed her, hurriedly throwing their skirts about them, and then with their stone knives severed branches and tied them together with deer thongs which they tore from the fringe of their girdles. On top of these they placed leafy branches and lifted the unconscious Cleopatra on to this improvised stretcher. In spite of their remonstrances, Pocahontas insisted upon taking one end of it, while the strongest two of her playmates bore the other.

Through the woods they walked, as silent now as they had been noisy before, but Pocahontas thought her heart-beats sounded as loud as the war drums of the Pamunkeys.

They were still distant many minutes' walk to the village when they caught sight of Pochins, a medicine man famous among many tribes for his powerful manitou, his guardian spirit, which enabled him to communicate with the manitous of the spirit world.

"Pochins, oh Pochins," cried out Pocahontas, "come and help us. I fear my sister is dying, and that I have killed her. She did not wish to go into the water, Pochins, and I pulled her in and now she hath cut her head and the blood floweth from it so that I can not stop it."

The shaman made no answer, but bent down from his great height and looked carefully at the wound, then he took the end of the stretcher from Pocahontas, saying:

"I will bear her to my prayer lodge here nearby."

Even then through the trees they caught sight of the bark covering of the lodge, which few persons had ever entered. The maidens shuddered at the sight of it, for none of them knew what mysterious terrors might lie in wait for them there. Nevertheless they followed Pochins as he bore Cleopatra inside and laid her on the ground. From an earthen bowl he took certain herbs and bound the leaves, after he had moistened them, over the wound. Soon Pocahontas, crouching at her sister's side, could see that the blood had ceased to flow. But no sign of life could be detected in the little body lying there. The hands and feet were clammy and though Pocahontas rubbed them vigorously, she could feel no warmth stirring in them.

The shaman paid, however, no further heed to her. From another bowl he took out a rattle of gourd, and from a peg on one of the rounded supports of the roof he lifted down a horrible mask painted in scarlet, and this he fastened over his face. Then, waving the children out of the way, he began to dance about the two sisters and to chant in a loud voice, shaking the rattle till it seemed as if the din must waken a dead person.

"My medicine is a mighty medicine," he exclaimed in his natural voice to Pocahontas. "Wait a little and thou shalt see what wonders it can do."

And indeed in a few moments Pocahontas felt the pulse start in her sister's arm, saw her eyelids quiver and her feet grow warm. And when the shouting and the shaking of the rattle grew even louder and more hideous, Cleopatra opened her eyes and looked about her in astonishment.

"Mighty indeed is the medicine (the magic) of Pochins," cried the shaman proudly as he laid aside mask and rattle; "it hath brought this maiden back from the dead."

Pocahontas now had to soothe the child, terrified by the sights she had seen and the sounds she had heard. She patted her arms and spoke to her as if she were a papoose on her back:

"Fear not, little one, no evil shall come to thee. Pocahontas watcheth over thee. She will not close her eyes while danger prowleth about. Fear naught, little one."

And Cleopatra clung to her, feeling a sense of security in her sister's fearlessness.

By this time the news of the accident had spread through the village and several squaws, led by Cleopatra's mother, came running to Pochins's lodge. Finding Cleopatra was able to rise, they carried her back with them. The other maidens, now the excitement was over, remembered their empty stomachs and hurried off to recover the dinner they had left behind at the waterfall.

Pocahontas did not go with them. She still sat on the ground beside the medicine man while he busied himself painting the mask where the color had worn off.

"Shaman," she asked, "tell me where went the manitou of my sister while she lay there dead?"

"On a distant journey," he answered; "therefore I had to call so loudly to make it hear me and return."

"Who taught thee thy medicine?" she questioned again.

"The Beaver, my manitou, daughter of Powhatan," he answered.

"And who then will teach me; how shall I learn?"

"Thou needest not such knowledge, since thou art neither a medicine man nor a brave. I, Pochins, will call to Okee, the Great Spirit, for thee when thou hast need of anything, food or raiment or a chief to take thee to his lodge."

"But I should like to do that myself, Pochins," she remonstrated. "Thou dost not know how many things I long to do myself. Let me put on thy mask and take thy rattle, just to see how they feel."

"Nay, nay, touch them not," he cried, stretching out his hand. "The Beaver would be angry with us and would work evil medicine on us."

Pochins was not fond of children. His dignity was so great that he never even noticed them as he strode through the village. But the eager look in Pocahontas's eyes seemed to draw words out of him. He began to talk to her of the many days and nights he had spent alone, fasting, in the prayer lodge until some message came to him from Okee, some message about the harvest or the success of a hunting party. Pocahontas was so interested that she asked him many questions.

"Tell me of Michabo, Michabo, the Great Hare," she coaxed, as she moved over on a mat Pochins had spread for her.

"Hearken, then, daughter of The Powhatan," he began, his voice changing its natural tone to one of chanting, "to the story of Michabo as it is told in the lodges of the Powhatans, the Delawares and of those tribes who dwell far away beyond our forests, away where abideth the West Wind and where the Sun strideth towards the darkness.

"Michabo dived down into the water when there was no land and no beast and no man or woman and he was lonely. From the bottom took he a grain of fine white sand and bore it safely in his hand in his journey upward through the dark waters. This he cast upon the waves and it sank not but floated like a tiny leaf. Then it spread out, circling round and round, wider and wider as the rings widen when thou casteth a stone into a still lake, till it had grown so large that a swift young wolf, though he ran till he dropped of old age, could not come to its ending. This earth rose all covered with trees and hills and beasts and men and women, and Michabo, the Great Hare, the Spirit of Light, the Great White One, hunted through earth's forests and he fashioned strong nets for fishing and he taught the stupid men, who knew naught, how to hunt also and to catch fish that they might not die of hunger.

"But Michabo had mightier deeds to do than the slaying of the fat deer or the netting of the salmon. His father was the mighty West Wind, Ningabiun, and he had slain his wife, the mother of Michabo. So when Michabo's grandmother had told him of the misdeeds of his father, Michabo rose up and called out to the four corners of the world: 'Now go I forth to slay the West Wind to avenge the death of my mother.'

"At last he found Ningabiun on the top of a high mountain, his cheeks puffed out and his headdress waving back and forth. At first they talked peacefully together and the West Wind told Michabo that only one thing in all the world could bring harm to him, and that was the black rock.

"'Wert thou the cause of my mother's death?' questioned Michabo, his eyes flashing, and Ningabiun calmly answered 'Yes.'

"So Michabo in his fury picked up a piece of black rock and struck at Ningabiun with all his might. A terrible conflict was this, such as hath never been seen since; the earth shook and the lightnings flashed down the sides of the mountain. So great was Michabo's strength that the West Wind was driven backwards. Over mountains and lakes Michabo drove him and across wide rivers, till they two came to the very brink of the world. Ningabiun feared that his son was going to push him off and cried out:

"Hold, my son, thou knowest not my power and that it is impossible to kill me. Desist and I will portion out to thee as much power as I have given to thy brothers. The four quarters of the globe are theirs, but thou canst do more than they, if thou wilt help the people of the earth. Go and do good, and thy fame will last forever.'

"So Michabo ceased from the battle and went down to help our fathers in the hunt and in the council and in the prayer-lodge; but to this day great cliffs of black rock show where Michabo strove with his father, the West Wind."

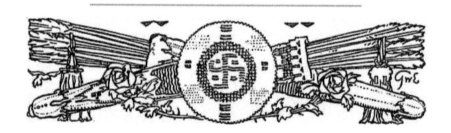

CHAPTER III

MIDNIGHT IN THE FOREST

Nautauquas, son of Powhatan, was returning at night through the forest towards his lodge at Werowocomoco. Over his shoulder hung the deer he had gone forth to slay. His mother had said to him:

"Thy leggings are old and worn, and thou knowest that good luck cometh to the hunter wearing moccasins and leggings made from skins of his own slaying. Go thou forth and kill a deer that I may soften its hide and make a covering of it for thy feet."

So Nautauquas had taken his bow and a quiver of arrows, and while Pocahontas and Cleopatra were sporting at the waterfall he had sought a pond whose surface was all but covered with fragrant water lilies, and he had hidden behind a sumac, bush, waiting patiently till a buck came down alone to drink. Only one arrow did he spend, which found its place between the wide branched antlers; then the hunter had waded into the pond, pushing aside the lily pads, and with one cut of his knife he had put an end to the struggling deer. Now he was bearing it home and he thought with eagerness of the savory meat it would yield him on the morrow. There was no doubt that he would have appetite ready for it, as all day long he had eaten nothing. It had been easy enough for him to have killed a squirrel and roasted it, but Nautauquas, knowing it was part of a brave's training to accustom himself to hunger, often fasted a long time voluntarily.

The night was a dark one, but now that the moon had risen, long vistas of light shone down the forest avenues, generally at that time so free from underbrush. Nautauquas, looking up through the branches at the moon, thought how it was the squaw of the sun and remembered the queer tales the old women were fond of relating about it.

Suddenly before him he saw a creature dancing down the moon-path, whirling and springing about while a pair of rabbits, that were startled in crossing the path, scurried off into a clump of sassafras bushes nearby. Then, as if reassured, they sat there calmly, even when the dancing figure came closer to them. And Nautauquas heard singing, though the words of the song did not come to his ears. He slipped behind an oak tree and watched the dancer advance. Now that it was nearer he discovered that it was a young girl; her only garment, a skirt of white buckskin, napped against her firm bare brown legs and a necklace of white shells clicked as she spun about. In the branches above some squirrels, awakened from their slumber, straightened their furry tails and began to chatter and a screech-owl tuwitted and tuwhoed. There was something familiar in the outlines, and Nautauquas was therefore not completely astonished when, turning about, she showed the face of Pocahontas.

"Matoaka," he cried, stepping from the shadow; "what dost thou here alone at night?"

His sister did not scream nor jump at this sudden interruption. She seized her brother's hand and pressed it gently.

"It was such a beautiful night, Nautauquas," she replied, "that I could not lie sleeping in the lodge. I come often here."

"And hast thou no fear, little sister?" he asked affectionately; "no fear of wild animals or of our enemies?"

"Wild animals will not hurt me. I patted a mother bear with cubs one night, and she did not even growl."

Nautauquas did not doubt her word. He knew that there were certain human beings whom beasts will not hurt.

"And enemies," she continued, "would not venture so near the village of the mighty Powhatan."

"I heard thee singing, little White Feather; what was thy song?"

"I made it many moons ago," she answered, "and I sing it always when I dance here at night. Listen then, thou shalt hear the song Matoaka, daughter of Powhatan, made to sing in the woods by Werowocomoco."

And she danced slowly, imitating with head and hands, body and feet, the words of her song.

I am the sister of the Morning Wind,And he and I awake the lazy Sun.We ruffle up the down of sleeping birds,And blow our laughter in the rabbits' ears,And bend the saplings till they kiss my feet,And the long grass till it obeisance makes.

I am the sister of the wan MoonbeamWho calls to me when I have fallen asleep:Come, see how I have witched the world in white.—So faint his voice no other ear can hear.And I steal forth from out my father's lodge,And of the world there only waketh IAnd bears and wildcats and the sly raccoonAnd deer from out whose eyes there look the soulsOf maidens who have died ere they knew love.And then the world we shorten with our feetThat wake no echoes, but the hornèd owlSigheth to think that thus our wingless speedAll but outdoes that of the tree-dwellers.

When she had finished she threw herself down at his feet, asking:

"Dost thou like my song, my brother?"

"Yes, it is a new song, Matoaka, and some day thou must sing it for our father. But it seemeth to me that thou art different from other maids. They do not care to rise from their sleeping mats and go forth alone into the forest."

"Perhaps they have not an arrow inside of them as have I."

Nautauquas had seated himself in the crotch of a dogwood-tree and looked with interest at his sister below him.

"An arrow?" he queried; "what dost thou mean?"

"I think," she answered, speaking slowly, "that within me is an arrow—not of wood and stone, but one of manitou—how shall I explain it to thee? I must go forth to distances, to deeds. I am shot forward by some bow and I may not hang idle in a quiver. I know," she continued, fingering the quiver on his back, "how thine own arrow feels after thou hast fashioned it carefully of strong wood and bound its head upon it with thongs. It says to itself; 'I am happy here, hanging in my warm bed on Nautauquas's back.' And then when thou takest it in thy hand and fittest its notch to the bowstring, it crieth out: 'Now I shall speed forth; now shall I cut the wind; now shall I journey where no arrow ever journeyed before; now shall I achieve what I was fashioned for!'"

"Strange thoughts are these, little sister, for a maid to think," and Nautauquas stroked the long braid against his knee.

"I am so happy, Nautauquas," she went on. "I love the warm lodge, the fire embers in the centre, the smoke curling up towards the stars I can see through the opening above me. I love to feel little Cleopatra's feet touching my head as we lie there together. But then I feel the arrow within me and I rise to my feet silently and creep out, and if the dogs hear me I whisper to them and they lie down quietly again. I love Werowocomoco, yet I long too to go beyond the village to where the sky touches the earth. I love the tales of the beasts the old squaws tell, but I want to hear the braves when they speak of war and ambushes. Springtime and the sowing of the corn are full of delight, yet I look forward eagerly to the earing of the corn and the fall of the leaf."

The maiden spoke passionately. So had she never spoken to anyone. She ceased for a moment and there was no sound save the call of the owl. Then she turned around and knelt, her elbows on her brother's knees, and asked:

"Tell me, Nautauquas, tell me the truth, since thou canst speak naught else; what manitou is in me that I am like to rushing water, to a stream that hurries forward? What shall I become?"

"Something great, Matoaka," he answered; "I know not whether a warrior—such there have been—a princess who shall hold many tribes in her hand, or a prophetess; but I am certain that the arrow of thy manitou shall bring down some fair game."

"Ah!" she breathed deeply. "I thank thee for thy words, Nautauquas, my brother, and that thou hast not made sport of me."

"Why should anyone make sport of thee? It is not strange that the aspen should quiver when the wind blows, nor that thou shouldst be swayed by the spirit that is within thee, Matoaka. Some day—"

He was interrupted by a piercing scream from the depth of the forest. He sprang to his feet; all the dreaminess of his attitude and mood had vanished; he pulled an arrow from his quiver fitted it to the string in readiness to shoot. Was it possible, he wondered, for any war party of their enemies to have ventured so near Powhatan's stronghold without having been halted at other villages belonging to his people? Pocahontas too was on her feet, her head on one side, listening intently.

Again came the scream, then Nautauquas loosened his bow, saying:

"That is no human cry. It is a wildcat in agony. Let us go and see what aileth it."

They ran swiftly towards the point from which the sound had come. Again came the cry to guide them, and then there was silence as they ran through the moonlight checkered by the shadows of the trees.

Nautauquas stood still suddenly, so suddenly that Pocahontas behind him could not stop quickly enough and fell against him and almost down into a ravine that lay beneath, but Nautauquas caught her on the very brink.

"It is down there," he pointed; "there must be a trap, I think. Let us descend very carefully."

They clambered down through the darkness made by the overhanging bushes and rocks. At the bottom the light was not obscured, and they beheld the striped body of a large wildcat caught in a trap.

"Look," cried Pocahontas excitedly, "there is another beast just there in those bushes. Our coming must have frightened it. He has been trying to kill the one in the trap, that cannot defend himself."

"That is so," assented Nautauquas, making ready to shoot the beast that was at liberty in case it should spring towards them. But the animal evidently had no taste that night for an encounter with human beings, and slouched off and up the side of the ravine. The imprisoned animal, they could see, was bleeding from a large wound on its back, and in the moonlight its eyes shone like fire.

"Poor beast!" exclaimed Nautauquas compassionately. "I would free him if he would let me touch him. As it is he will have to starve to death unless his enemy comes back to finish him."

"No," said Pocahontas, "that need not be. I will loose him and bind up his wound if thou wilt cut a strip off thy leggings."

"Silly child," he laughed. "A wild beast needs no balsam nor cloths for his wounds. If he were free to drag himself to safety he would lick his hurt till it healed. But he would bite thy hand off shouldst thou attempt to touch him."

"Nay, Nautauquas, he would not harm me. See how quiet he will grow."

She knelt down just beyond the reach of the wildcat and began to whisper to it. Nautauquas could not make out what she said, but to his amazement he beheld how the beast ceased to lash its tail and how its muscles seemed to relax. Nevertheless the young brave caught Pocahontas by the arm and tried to pull her away.

"There is no danger, my brother," she remonstrated. "Fear not. Hast thou not seen old Father Noughmass when the bees swarm over his neck and hands? They never sting him. He cannot tell thee why, nor do I know why wild beasts will not harm me."

So Nautauquas, knife in hand and breathing deeply, looked on while Pocahontas, speaking words in a low voice, moved nearer and nearer the wildcat. Taking her knife from her girdle, she began to cut through the thongs that held him. One paw was now loose and yet the beast did not move to touch his rescuer. Then when the other thongs were loose and it was free, it moved off slowly and painfully into the woods as if no human beings were there.

Nautauquas breathed a sigh of relief.

"It is wonderful, Matoaka, yet I pray thee test thy strange power not too far. I am glad though the poor beast got away. I like not to see them suffer. I shoot and kill for food and for skins, but I kill at once."

They now climbed up the ravine again and started off in the direction of Werowocomoco.

The night was already far advanced and Pocahontas was growing drowsier and drowsier. Nautauquas, seeing that she was almost asleep, took hold of her arm and made her lean on him. As they approached the spot where he had first come across her dancing, they noticed a human figure crouched on the ground. Even in the moonlight, grown dimmer as dawn approached, he could see that it was an old squaw. Pocahontas recognized old Wansutis, a gatherer of herbs and roots.

"What dost thou here, Wansutis?" she questioned.

"He! the little princess," cried the old woman, scowling up at them, "and the young brave Nautauquas. I seek roots and leaves by the light of the Sun's squaw. So is it meet for me and so will the drinks be stronger when brewed by old Wansutis. I have found many rare plants this night; it hath been a lucky one, perchance because the young princess was also abroad in the forest."

All the children of the tribe were afraid of the old woman. They told each other tales of how she could turn those she disliked into dogs, bats or turtles. And now even Nautauquas remembered how he had run from her when he was a little fellow. Her expression was so ugly and so malign that Pocahontas, though she did not fear her exactly, had no desire to stay longer, and so started forward.

"And what doth Pocahontas in the woods at night?" asked Wansutis. "Knoweth The Powhatan that she hath left his lodge?"

Pocahontas, though she often willingly allowed those about her to forget her rank, could yet be very conscious of it when she desired. Now it did not please her to be questioned in this manner by the old squaw and she did not answer.

"Oh hey," cried Wansutis, "thou wilt not answer me. Thou art proud of thy rank and thy youth. Yet one day thou wilt be an old squaw like me, without teeth, with weak legs, and life a burden to thee. Then thou wilt not be so proud."

Pocahontas stopped and turned around again.

"Nay, I will not grow old. I will not let the day come when life shall be a burden. Thou canst not read the future, Wansutis. I shall always be as fleet as now."

"Thinketh thou to ward off old age by some of my potions made from these roots I carry here, a bundle too heavy for an ancient crone like me to bear on her back? Thou shalt have none of them."

At these words Pocahontas's manner changed. Stooping, she picked up the bundle and pressed it into the net that lay on the ground and swung it on to her strong shoulders.

"Come, Wansutis," she cried. "Seek not to anger me with words and I will bear thy bundle to thy wigwam. It is in truth too heavy for thy old bones."

The old woman grunted ungraciously as she rose to her feet, then the three, one following the other, moved forward. They were obliged to go slowly, as Wansutis could only hobble along, and Nautauquas was sorry to see that dawn was approaching. He feared now that Pocahontas would not be able to steal unobserved back to her place beside Cleopatra and that she would be scolded. They went with Wansutis to her wigwam and Pocahontas let fall her bundle. Nautauquas took out his knife and cut off a hind quarter of the deer and laid it on the squaw's hearth.

"She hath no son to hunt for her," he said in explanation as he and Pocahontas went off unthanked.

Wansutis's wigwam was on the edge of the village. As they came nearer to the lodges they heard yelling and shouting from every side, and they saw small boys and young braves rush forth, glancing eagerly about them.

"Let us hasten," cried Pocahontas. "I wonder what hath befallen, Nautauquas."

CHAPTER IV

RUNNING THE GAUNTLET

"What hath happened?" Nautauquas called out to Parahunt, his brother, when he caught up with him hastening to the river.

"Word hath come by a runner that one of the tribes from the Chickahominy villages hath fallen upon a party of Massawomekes and hath vanquished them. Even now they are approaching with the prisoners."

In passing the front of his wigwam Nautauquas threw down the carcass of the deer, then ran on to join the ever increasing crowd of braves and children on the river bank.

Pocahontas too had mingled in the throng, and so Cleopatra and the squaws in the lodge had not noticed her absence, thinking when they saw her that she had been roused from sleep in the early dawn as they had been.

It was now almost light. Far down the river six large dugouts were approaching. But even that sight was not sufficient to make the onlookers forget the fact that the sun was rising and must be greeted with the customary ceremony. Two chiefs, whose duty it was, took from their pouches handfuls of dried uppowoc (tobacco), and each turning away from the other, walked in a large half-circle, scattering the uppowoc upon the ground, until when they met a brown ring had been formed. Within this braves and squaws hurried to seat themselves. With uplifted eyes and outstretched hands they greeted the Sun who had come back to them to warm their fields and to draw their young corn upright.

By the time this morning ceremony was over the dugouts were almost at the beach. There was now a great shouting and yelling from shore to boats and from boats to shore, and Pocahontas slipped into a thicket of bushes on to a higher point of the bank where she could be alone to watch the landing. She clapped her hands as their friends, the stalwart Chickahominies, leaped ashore, twenty to each huge dugout; and though her dignity would not permit her to call out derisively, as did the crowd, to the three prisoners each boat contained, she looked eagerly to see what kind of monsters these enemies of her tribe might be.

The eighteen Massawomekes were not bound; they stepped from the dugouts as firmly as if they were going to a feast instead of to torture. They were of the Iroquois nation; and Pocahontas, who had heard many stories of this race, always at enmity with her own, noticed certain differences in the way they were tattooed and in the shape of their headdresses.

Victors and prisoners, followed by the crowd, marched forward to the ceremonial lodge where The Powhatan was awaiting them. Pocahontas slipped into the already crowded space, though one of Powhatan's squaws tried to stay her. She made her way without further opposition between Chickahominies and Massawomekes, up to the dais where her father sat, and crouched down on a mat spread on raised hurdles at his feet, where she could observe all that went on.

One of the Chickahominy chiefs, whose face she remembered to have seen at the great autumn festivals, was the first to speak:

"Powhatan, ruler of two hundred villages and lord of thirty tribes, who rulest from the salt water to the western forests, we come to tell thee how we have pursued thine enemies, the Massawomekes, who two months ago did slay in ambush a party of our young men out hunting deer. By the Great Swamp (the Dismal Swamp of Virginia) we came upon them, and though they sought like bears to hide themselves in its secret places, lo! I, Water Snake, did track them and I and my braves fell upon them, and now they are no more."

Murmurs of assent and of approval were heard throughout the lodge. The prisoners alone were apparently as unconscious of Water Snake's recital as if they were still hidden in the fastnesses of the Great Swamp.

"There where we fought," continued the orator, waving his hand towards the southwest, "the white blossoms of the creeping plants turned crimson, and the hungry buzzards circled overhead. Many a Massawomeke squaw sits to-night in a lonely wigwam; many a man child among them hath lost the father to teach him how to bend a bow. We slew them all, Great Werowance, all but these captives we have brought before thee."

This time louder shouts of approval rewarded Water Snake's speech, which did not cease until it was seen that Powhatan meant to acknowledge it. He did not rise nor change his position in any way, and his voice was low and measured.

"A tree hath many branches, but one trunk only. Deep into the earth stretch its roots to suck up nourishment for every twig and leaf. I, Wahunsunakuk, Chief of the Powhatans and many tribes, am the trunk, and one of my many branches is that of the Chickahominies and one that is very close to my heart. My children have done well and the Powhatan thanks them for their brave deeds. Now can your young braves go forth upon the hunt unharmed and bring back meat for feastings and hides for their squaws to fashion."

He paused and all the eyes of his people in the lodge were bent on him with the same question.

"My children ask of me 'What shall we do with these captives?' and I make answer, feast them first, that they may not say that the Powhatans are greedy and give not to strangers. Then when they have feasted let them run the gauntlet."

He waved his hand in token that he had finished speaking, and the glad news was shouted from the lodge to the eager crowd without. Pocahontas knew as well as if she could see them that the squaws were hurrying about to prepare the food, and from her low seat she could see between the legs of the braves before her how a number of boys were lying on their stomachs, trying to wriggle into the lodge that they might hear for themselves the interesting things going on and observe for themselves whether the captives showed any sign of fear.

Now Powhatan gave an order and all seated themselves on the ground or on mats in lines facing him. Then in came the squaws bearing large wooden and grass-woven dishes of food. There were hot cakes of maize and wild turkeys and fat raccoons. The captives were served first and none of them refused. They would not let their enemies believe that fear of their coming fate could spoil their appetites. So, after throwing the first piece of meat into the fire as an offering to Okee, they ate eagerly.

One of them who sat nearest the front, Pocahontas noticed, was but little older than herself. He was too young to be a brave; perhaps, she thought, he had run off from home and had followed the war party, as she had heard of boys in her own tribe doing. She wondered if now he was regretting that his eagerness for adventure had made his first warpath his last one.

When they had feasted the squaws passed around bunches of turkey feathers for them to wipe their greasy fingers on, and in every way the captives were treated with that exaggerated courtesy that was customary towards those about to be tortured.

Then Powhatan rose, and, preceded and followed by several of his fifty armed guards chosen from the tallest men of his thirty tribes, he strode down the centre of the lodge and out into the sunshine. Pocahontas walked next behind him, and once outside, ran to tell the curious Cleopatra all she had witnessed.

"Why shouldst thou have seen it all?" asked her jealous sister of Pocahontas, "while I had naught of it all but the shouting?"

"Because," laughed Pocahontas, pulling her sister's long hair, "because my two feet took me in. Thine are too fearful, little mouse."

An open space stretched before the ceremonial lodge, used for games and feats of running and shooting at a mark. Now Powhatan and his guard and his sons seated themselves upon the firm red ground that rose in a little hillock to a height of several feet at one side of the lodge. Then other chieftains took up their places behind them, standing or sitting; the squaws crowded in among them and the boys sought the branches of a single walnut-tree, the only tree within the limits of Werowocomoco. They looked with longing eyes at the slanting roof of the great lodge. That was undoubtedly the point of vantage, but The Powhatan was a much dreaded werowance and they dared not risk his ire.

Pocahontas, who had been wondering where to bestow herself, noticed the envying glances they cast in its direction. She was not withheld by their restraining fear, so running to the opposite side of the lodge, she climbed its sides, finding foothold in its bark covering, and soon was curled up comfortably, her hands about her knees, where she would miss nothing of the spectacle.

Now she beheld two long rows of young braves, one of them composed of Powhatans, the other of Chickahominies, stride down the open space below her and form a lane of naked, painted human walls. In their hands they held bunches of fresh green reeds, sharp as knives, or heavy bludgeons of oak, or stone tomahawks. For a moment they stood there motionless as if they were merely spectators of some drama to be enacted by others.

Pocahontas recognized most of them: Black Arrow, whose ear had been clawed off by a bear; Leaping Sturgeon, who had hung two scalps at his girdle before the chiefs had pronounced him old enough to be a brave; her own cousin, White Owl, the most wonderfully tattooed of them all; and the Nansamond young chieftain who wore a live snake as an earring in the slit of his ear.

Then Powhatan gave the signal and the captives were led forward. They knew what awaited them; probably each of them, except the young boy, had himself meted out the same fate to others that was now to befall them. They did not repine; it was the fortune of war. Singing songs of triumph, of derision of all their enemies, they started to run down the awful lane of death. Blows rained upon them, on neck, on head, on arms, even on their legs from stooping adversaries. So swift came the blows from both sides that sometimes two fell upon the same spot almost at once.

Pocahontas marked with interest that the boy was last of the line, and that he bore himself as bravely as the others.

When they reached the end of the row there was no escape—no escape anywhere more for them. Back they darted, so swiftly that it seemed as if each escaped the blow aimed at himself, only to receive the one meant for his comrade ahead.

Pocahontas had a queer feeling as she looked down on them and saw the blood spurting from a hundred wounds. She thought perhaps it was the hot sun that made her feel a little sick. Her eyes followed the boy and as he came nearer she noticed that he was almost at the end of his strength. A few more blows would finish him. Already some of his elders had fallen to the ground, and if, when beaten unmercifully, they were still unable to rise, the tomahawk dashed out their brains.

To her astonishment, Pocahontas found herself wishing the boy might not fall, might escape in some miraculous manner. What a wrong thought! she said to herself: was he not an enemy of her tribe? Yet she could not help closing her eyes when she saw Black Arrow aiming a terrible blow at his head. She did not know what to make of herself. She suddenly began to think of the hurt wild-cat she and Nautauquas had pitied during the night. But no one ought ever to pity an enemy. What was she made of?

As she opened her eyes again she heard a woman's outcry and beheld a squaw rushing towards the end of the line where Black Arrow's blow had felled the boy. It was old Wansutis.

"I claim the boy," she panted; "I claim him by our ancient right. Cease, braves, and let me have him."

The astounded braves let their arms drop at their sides, and the panting, bleeding captives who had not already fallen, breathed for a moment long breaths.

"I claim the boy," the old woman cried again in a loud voice, turning towards Powhatan, "to adopt as a son. Many popanows (winters) and seed times have passed since my sons were slain. Now is Wansutis old and feeble and hath need of a young son to hunt for her. By our ancient custom this captive is mine."

There was an outcry of opposition from the younger braves at being robbed of one of their victims, but the older chiefs on the hill debated for a few moments, and then gave their decision: there was no doubt of the old woman's right to claim the boy. So Powhatan sent two of his guards to fetch him and to carry him to Wansutis's lodge.

Pocahontas suddenly felt at ease again. Yes, she couldn't help it, she said to herself, but she was glad the boy had not been beaten to pieces. As soon as he was carried off the running of the gauntlet began again. But Pocahontas had now had enough of it. It would continue, she knew, until all of the captives were dead. She slid down from the back of the lodge and led by curiosity, set off for Wansutis's wigwam. It was at the edge of the village, and before the slow procession of the two guards, the old woman and the boy had arrived, Pocahontas had hidden herself behind a mossy rock, from which hiding place she had a view right into the opening of the wigwam.

She watched the guards lay the unconscious boy gently down and Wansutis as she knelt and blew upon the embers under the smoke hole till they blazed up. Then she saw the old woman take a pot of water and heat it and throw herbs into it. With this infusion she bathed the wounds, anointing them afterwards with oil made from acorns. And while she worked she prayed, invoking Okee to heal her son, to make him strong that he might care for her old age.

Pocahontas was so eager to know whether the boy were alive that she crept closer to the wigwam, and when at last he opened his eyes they looked beyond the hearth and the crouching Wansutis, straight into those of Pocahontas. She saw that he had regained his senses, so she put her fingers to her lips. She did not want Wansutis to know that she had been watched. Already the touch of the wrinkled fingers was as tender as that of a mother, and Pocahontas felt sure that she would resent any intrusion. Now that she had seen all there was to see, she stole away.

After wandering through the woods to gather honeysuckle to make a wreath, she returned to the village. There was no longer a crowd in the open space; the captives were all dead and the spectators had gone to their various lodges. Only a number of boys were playing run the gauntlet, some with willow twigs beating those chosen by lot to run between them. A girl, imitating old Wansutis, rushed forward and claimed one of the runners for a son.

A few days later when the young Massawomeke lad had recovered there were ceremonies to celebrate his adoption as a member of the Powhatan tribe, of the great nation of the Algonquins. The other boys of his age looked up to him with envy. Had he not proved his valor on the warpath and under torture while they were only gaming with plumpits? They followed him about, eager to do his bidding, each trying to outdo his comrades in sports when his eye was on them. And all the elders had good words to say about Claw-of-the-Eagle, and Wansutis was so proud that she now often forgot to speak evil medicine.

Pocahontas wondered how Claw-of-the-Eagle liked his new life, and one day when she was running through the forest she came upon him. He had knelt to look through a thicket at a flock of turkeys he meant to shoot into, but his bow lay idle beside his feet, and she saw that his eyes seemed to be looking at something in the distance.

"What dost thou behold, son of Wansutis?" she asked.

He started but did not reply.

"Speak, Claw-of-the-Eagle," she said impatiently. "Powhatan's daughter is not wont to wait for a reply."

He saw that it was the same face he had beheld peering into the lodge at the moment he regained consciousness.

"I see the sinking sun. Princess of many tribes, the sun that journeys towards the mountains to the village whence I came."

"But thou art of us now," she rejoined.

"Yes, I am son of old Wansutis and I am loyal to my new mother and to my new people. And yet. Princess, I send each day a message by the sun to the lodge where they mourn Claw-of-the-Eagle. Perhaps it will reach them."

"Tell me of the mountains and of the ways of thy father's people. I long to learn of strange folk and different customs."

"Nay, Princess, I will not speak of them. Thou hast never bidden farewell to thy kindred forever. I would forget, not remember."

And Pocahontas, although it was almost the first time that any one had refused to obey her, was not angry. She was too occupied as she walked homeward wondering how it would seem if she were never to see Werowocomoco and her own people again.

CHAPTER V

THE GREAT BIRDS

Opechanchanough, brother of Wahunsunakuk, The Powhatan, had sent to Werowocomoco a boat full of the finest deep sea oysters and crabs. The great werowance had returned his thanks to his brother and the bearers of his gifts were just leaving when Pocahontas rushed in to her father's lodge half breathless with eagerness.

"Father," she cried, "I pray thee grant me this pleasure. It hath grown warm, and I and my maidens long for the cool air that abideth by the salty water. Therefore, I beseech thee, let us go to mine uncle for a few days' visit."

Powhatan did not answer at once. He did not like to have his favorite child leave him. But she, seeing that he was undecided, began to plead, to whisper in his ears words of affection and to stroke his hair till he gave his consent. Then Pocahontas ran off to get her long mantle and her finest string of beads and to summon the maidens who were to accompany her. They embarked in the dugout with her uncle's people and were rowed swiftly down the river.

At Kecoughtan they were received with much ceremony, for Pocahontas knew what was due her and how, when it was necessary, to put aside her childish manner for one more dignified. Opechanchanough greeted her kindly.

"Hast thou forgiven me, my uncle?" she asked as they sat down to a feast of the delicious little fish she always begged for when she visited him, and to steaks of bear meat; "hast thou forgiven the arrow I shot at thee last popanow?"

"I will remember naught unpleasant against thee, little kinswoman," he replied as he drank his cup of walnut milk.

"Indeed I am ashamed of my foolishness," continued his niece. "I was but a child then."

"And now?—it is but a few moons ago."

"But see how I grow, as the maize after a rain storm. Soon they will say I am ready for suitors."

"And whom wilt thou choose, Pocahontas?"

"I do not know. I have no thoughts for that yet."

"What then are thy thoughts of?"

"Of everything, of flowers and beasts, dancing and playing, of wars and ceremonies, of the new son of old Wansutis, of Nautauquas's new bow, of necklaces and earrings, of old stories and new songs—and of to-morrow's bathing."

"Fear not that thou hast yet left thy childhood behind thee," said her uncle.

Then when the fire died down and the storyteller's voice had grown drowsy, Pocahontas fell asleep, her arm resting on a baby bear that had been taken away from its dead mother and that would cuddle close to the person who lay nearest the fire.

Opechanchanough had not the same deep affection for children as that which Powhatan showed to his sons and daughters. He was as brave a fighter but not as great a leader in peace as Wahunsunakuk. It irked him that he had to give way to his brother and that he must obey his commands; yet he knew that only by unity between the different tribes of the seacoast could they be safe from their common enemies, the Iroquois. His vanity was very great and he had felt hurt at the ridicule which Pocahontas had caused to fall upon him. Had she come on her visit sooner he had surely not received her so kindly. But now there were other strange happenings and more important matters to consider, and he was too wise a chief to worry long over a child's pranks. Besides, he had learned, from his own observance and from the tongues of others, how his brother cherished her more than any of his squaws or children. So policy as well as his native hospitality dictated a kindly reception.

In the morning after they had eaten, Opechanchanough offered to send Pocahontas and her maidens in a canoe down to where a cape jutted out into the ocean that they might see the breakers at their highest, but Pocahontas declined.

"Nay, Uncle," she said, "but my maidens have never seen the sea. They be stay-at-homes and I would not affright them too sorely by the sight of mountains of water. Have no care for us save to bid some one supply us with food to take along. I know the way down to a smooth beach where we can disport ourselves."

So Opechanchanough, relieved to have them off his hands, let her have her will.

The town was within a mile of open water, and the maidens started off with a large supply of dried flesh slung in osier baskets on their backs. Some of the young braves looked after them as they went and disputed as to which of them they would like to choose as squaw when they were older.

Pocahontas led the way through wild rose bushes and sumac, with here and there an occasional tall pine tree, its lowest branches high above their heads. They were all of them in the gayest humor: it was a day made for pleasure, and they had not a care in the world. They sang as they walked and joked each other, Pocahontas herself not escaping.

"Did the bear, thy bedfellow, scratch thee?" asked one, "and didst thou outdo him, for this morning he was not to be found near the lodge."

"Perhaps," suggested another, "it was not a real bear cub but some evil manitou."

The maidens shuddered deliciously at this possibility.

"Nonsense," called back Pocahontas, "he was real enough; here is the mark of one claw on my foot. Besides, I do not believe the evil manitou can have such power on such a beautiful day as this. Okee must have bid them fly away."

Now suddenly the path turned and before them shone the silver mirror of the sea.

"Behold!" cried Pocahontas, and then Red Wing, her nearest companion, fell flat upon the ground, burying her face in the sand. The others stood and stared at the new watery world in front of them, hushed in an awed silence. Gradually their curiosity got the better of their fear and they began to question:

"How many leagues does it stretch, Pocahontas?"—"Can war canoes find their way on it?"—"Come the good oysters from its depths?" asked Deer-Eye, whose appetite was always made fun of.

Pocahontas answered as well as she was able, but to her who had seen several times before the great water, it was almost as much of a mystery as to her comrades. But to-day she greeted it as an old friend. She could scarcely wait to throw herself into the little rippling waves at her feet.

"Come on," she cried, "let us hasten. How wonderful to our heated bodies will its freshness be." And as she ran towards it she threw off her skirt, her moccasins and her necklace and dashed into the sea.

Though her companions were used to swimming from the day their mothers had thrown them as babies into the river to harden them, they had never been where there were not protecting banks on each side of them, and they were afraid to follow Pocahontas into this unknown. But gradually her evident safety and delight were too much for their caution, and they were soon at home in the gentle waves.

For nearly an hour they played their water games, chasing and ducking each other, racing and swimming underneath the surface. Then they grew hungry and bethought themselves of their food waiting to be cooked. But when they were on the shore again and about to start a fire to heat their meat, Pocahontas bade them wait.

"Here," she said, "is fresher food. See what the tide has left for us."

To their great astonishment the maidens, who did not know the sea retreated, saw how while they were bathing the water had bared the sand, leaving it full of little pools. Standing in one of them, Pocahontas stooped down and ran her hand through the mud, bringing up a soft-shelled crab.

"See," she cried, "there are hundreds of them for our dinner, but be careful to hold them just so, that they may not nip you."

And her maidens, laughing and shrieking, soon had a larger supply of crabs than they could eat. They found bits of wood on the beach and dried sea weed which they set on fire by twirling a pointed stick in a wooden groove they had brought along with their food. After they had eaten, they stretched out lazily on the sand and talked until they began to doze off, one by one.

Pocahontas had strolled a little further down the beach, picking up the fine thin shells of transparent gold and silver which she liked to make into necklaces. She had found a number of them and as they were more than she could hold in her hands, she sat down to string them on a piece of eel grass until she could transfer them to a thread of sinew. When she had finished she lay back against a ridge of sand and watched the gulls as they flew above her, dipping down into the waves every now and then to bring up a fish. Far away a school of porpoises was circling the waves, their black fins sinking out of sight and reappearing as regularly as if they moved to some marine music. Pocahontas wondered whence they came and whither they and the gulls were bound. How delightful it was to move so rapidly and so easily through water or air. But she did not think of envying them. Was she not as fleet as they in her element? She pressed her hand against the warm sand how she loved the feel of it; she stretched her naked foot to where the little waves could wet it. How she loved the lapping of the water! Within her was a welling up of feeling, a love for all things living.

It was a very quiet world just now; the sun was only a little over the zenith. Only the cries of the sea gulls and the soft swish of the waves broke the silence. It would be pleasant to sleep here as her comrades were sleeping, but if she slept then she would miss the consciousness of her enjoyment.

Yet, though she intended to keep awake, when she looked seaward, she felt sure that she must have fallen asleep and was dreaming the strangest of dreams. For nowhere save in dreamland had anyone ever beheld such a sight as seemed to stand out against the horizon. Three great birds, that some shaman had doubtless created with powerful medicine, so large that they almost touched the heavens, were skimming the waves, their white wings blown forward. One, much larger than the others, moved more swiftly than they.

Yet never, in a dream or in life, were such birds, and little Pocahontas, who had sprung to her feet, stood gaping in terrified wonder.

"Then must I be bewitched!" she cried aloud; "some evil medicine hath befallen me."

She called out, and there was a tone in her voice that roused the sleeping maidens as a war drum roused their fathers.

"What see ye?" she asked anxiously.

"Oh! Pocahontas, we know not," they answered in terror, huddling about her; "answer *thou* us. What are those strange things that speed over the waves? Whence come they—from the rim of the world?"

Pocahontas, the fearless, was frightened. She gave one more glance seaward, and then turning, took to her heels in terror. Her maidens, who had never seen her thus, added her fright to they own, and none stopped until they had reached the lodge at Kecoughtan.

The squaws rushed out when they caught sight of the frightened children and tried to soothe them, but they could get no explanation of what had startled them. Finally Opechanchanough strode out, and when Pocahontas had tried to tell him what she had seen his face grew stern.

"It is as I feared," he said to another chief. "And so the word which came from the upper cape was true. It is a marvel that bodeth no good."

He began to give orders hurriedly; the dugout was brought up to the landing, and he waved Pocahontas and her maidens in with scant ceremony.

"I will send a runner to Werowocomoco with news to my brother," he called out to her as the boat was swung out into the river; "he will reach the village by land more quickly than by river. Farewell, Matoaka."

And Pocahontas, though she longed to have questioned him in regard to what he had heard and feared, yet rejoiced that she was on her way to her people, to her home where such strange sights as she had just beheld never came.

CHAPTER VI

JOHN SMITH'S TEMPTATION

The *Discovery*, the *Godspeed* and the *Susan Constant*, after nearly five months of tossing about upon the seas, were now swinging at anchor in the broad mouth of the River James, which the loyal English adventurers had named after their king. The white sails that had so terrified the Indian maidens now flapped against the masts, having fully earned their idleness. On board the discussion still continued as to the best situation for the town they designed to be the first permanent English settlement in America—in Wingandacoa, as the land was called before the name Virginia was given to it in honour of Queen Elizabeth, "The Virgin Queen."

The expedition had set out from England in December of the year before (1606). Among those who filled the three ships were men already veteran explorers and others who had never been a day's voyage away from their island home.

Among the former were Bartholomew Gosnold, who had first sailed for the strange new world some five years before. He had landed far to the north of the river where the ships now rested—on a colder, sterner shore. There he had discovered and named Cape Cod and Martha's Vineyard. Christopher Newport too had sailed before in Western waters, but further to the southward. He was an enemy of the Spaniard wherever he found him, and had left a name of terror through the Spanish Main, for had he not sacked four of their towns in the Indies and sunk twenty Spanish galleons? And there was John Smith, who had fought so many battles in his twenty-seven years that many a graybeard soldier could not cap his tales of sieges, sword-play, imprisonment and marvelous escapes. And many other men were there whom hope of gain or love of adventure had brought across the Atlantic. They had listened to the strange story of the lost colony on Roanoke Island, English men and women killed doubtless by the Indians, though no sure word of their fate was ever to be known, but fear of a like destiny had not deterred them from coming.

There were many points to be considered: The settlement must be near the coast, so that the ships from home would be able to reach it with as little delay as possible, yet away from the coast in case of raids by the Spaniards.

Again, the location must be healthful, and quite easily defended, for the attack by the natives upon the colonists when they first landed at the cape they called Henry after the young Prince of Wales, had given them a taste of what they might have to expect. It was the rumor of this fight which had reached Opechanchanough at Kecoughtan.

At the prow of the *Discovery* stood a man who paid no attention to the disputes going on behind him. He was not tall, but was powerfully built, and even the sight of his back would have been sufficient to prove him a man accustomed to a life of action. It was not so easy, however, to guess at his age. His long beard and mustache hid his mouth, and there were deep lines from his nose downward that might have been marked by years. Yet his brow was high and wide and unfurrowed, and his hair was abundant and his eyebrows dark and high. An intelligent, eager countenance it was, of a man who had seen more of the world in his short twenty-eight years than any white-haired octogenarian of his native Lincolnshire. He held a spy glass and, standing by the rail, moved it slowly until he had pointed it in every direction. He had swept the river and both shores as far as his eye could reach and now it rested on an island some little distance above, near the right-hand bank of the newly named river.

A sailor, pushing through the crowd about the cabin door, approached the man at the prow.

"Captain Smith," he said, "Captain Newport bids me say that the Council is about to be sworn in in the cabin and that he desires thy presence there."

John Smith turned and walked slowly aft, wondering what would be decided in the next hour. Was he, who felt within himself an unusual power to organize and to command men, to be given this wonderful chance, such as never yet had come to an Englishman, to plant firmly in a new land the seed of a great colony? From his early youth his days had been devoted to adventure. He was of that race of Englishmen who first discovered how small were the confines of their little island and who sallied gaily forth to seek new worlds for their ambition and energy. Raleigh, Drake, Sir Martin Frobisher, Sir Humphry Gilbert, Sir Richard Grenville and John Smith were the scouts sent out by England's genius to discover the pathways along which she was to send her sons. Bold, fearless, untiring, cruel often, at other times kind and firm, they went into new seas and lands, seeking a Northwest Passage, or to "singe the beard of the King of Spain," or to find the legendary treasures of the New Indies—yet all of them were serving unconsciously the genius of their race in laying the foundations of new worlds. Perhaps of them all Smith saw most clearly the value of the settlement in Virginia, and just as clearly was he aware that the jealousies and avarice of many of his fellow colonists would threaten seriously its growth and indeed its very existence.

Though not one among the curious eyes turned on him, as he walked slowly towards the stem, beheld any trace of emotion on his grave face, he was consumed with the hope that he might be chosen to lead the great work. Yet he feared, knowing that all the long voyage, almost from the time they had sailed from England, his enemies, jealous of his fame and of his power over men, had sought to undermine it and to slander his good name. What lies they had spread through the three ships of a mutiny he was said to be instigating, until orders were passed which made him virtually a prisoner for the rest of the journey. But he would soon find out if they intended to disregard and pass him by.

"WE CHOOSE TODAY," HE CRIED

When he entered the little cabin he saw seated along the transom and in the wide-armed chairs Captain Christopher Newport, Bartholomew Gosnold, Edward Wingfield, John Ratcliffe, John Martin and George Kendall. They greeted Smith as he entered, as did the other gentlemen leaning against the bulkheads, but with no cordiality, and he knew well that they had been talking of him before he entered. He took his seat in silence.

These men composed the Council which had been designated in the secret instructions given them when they sailed and opened after they had passed between Capes Charles and Henry. And this Council now it was which, according to its right, was to elect their president for the year to come. Smith now felt certain that owing to their hostility to him they had already determined among themselves what their votes should be while he was without the cabin. The form, however, was gone through with and the result solemnly announced: Wingfield was to be the first president of the Colony, and Smith found himself not even mentioned for the smallest office. The others for the most part smiled with pleasure as they looked to see his disappointment, but he showed none. Instead he rose to his feet and said:

"Captain Newport and gentlemen of the Council, will ye let me suggest for the name of this new colony that of our gracious sovereign, King James."

Here at last they must follow his lead, and all sprang to their feet and shouted "Jamestown let it be!"

Then began again the discussion of the spot to be chosen for their settlement. There were those who desired a site nearer the bay; one advocated exploring the other rivers in the vicinity, the Apamatuc, the Nansamond, the Chickahominy, the Pamunkey, as the Indians called them, before deciding; but Newport, eager to return to England, would not consent.

"We choose to-day," he cried, bringing his fist down on the table with a bang.

The island that Smith had been examining with his glass was considered. It was large and level and not too far from the sea, said one in its favor. The majority were for it and the others were at last brought round to their point of view. Smith had not put forward any suggestions. He knew whatever he advocated would have been voted down. When asked what he thought of the island his answer, "It hath much to commend it," left his hearers still in doubt as to his real choice.

"Now that we have christened the babe before it is born," said Captain Newport, rising, "let us ashore and get to work to mark out the site of our Jamestown."

All left the ship with the exception of a few sailors who remained on guard. After more discussion the Council picked out the spots for the government house, for the church, for the storehouse, while the artisans busied themselves with no loss of time in cutting down trees and clearing spaces for the temporary tents. The matter of a fort had not been broached, yet Smith, whose military knowledge showed him how vulnerable the island was, made no suggestion for its fortification.

He had strolled alone through the tangle of undergrowth, of flowering vines in which frightened mocking-birds and catbirds were darting, to the side of the island nearest the bank of the mainland.

"Here," he said, speaking aloud as he had learned to do when he was a captive among the Tartars that he might not forget the sound of his own tongue, "here, on this side should be a bastioned wall with some strong culverins. A lookout tower at this corner and, extending around north and south, a strong palisade—that with vigilant sentries would ensure against attack except by water. If I—"

Then he stopped, his brow knitting. His disappointment had been a keen one, his pride was smitten to the quick. Never had he left England, never thrown in his lot with the new colony, had he known how he was to be made to suffer from jealousy, intrigue and neglect. As he stood gazing across into the deeper tangle on the opposite shore his thoughts were occupied with decisions for his future.

"Why should I remain here," he cried aloud, "to be disregarded, when there is many an English ship that would be fain to have me stand on her poop, many a company of yeomen that would be main glad to have me command them? I am not of those men who are wont always to follow orders. I am made to *give* them. The world's wide and this island need not be my prison. I will sail back on the *Discovery* and e'en be on the lookout for some new adventures."

A rustling in the bushes behind him made him turn quickly. There stood Dickon and Hugh and Hob, three of the men who had come from his own part of the country, with whom during the long voyage he had often been glad to chat of their homes and the folk they all knew.

"Captain," spake Dickon, "we have followed to have a word wi' thee in secret. 'Tis said they have not given thee a place in the Council. Is't true?"

"Aye," answered Smith calmly.

"'Tis a dirty trick," cried Hugh, and his comrades echoed him. "A dirty trick, but what wilt thou do now?"

"What would ye have me do, men?" asked Smith curiously.

Dickon was again spokesman, the others nodding approval of his words.

"We be thy friends, Captain, and thy wellwishers. We came to this strange land to make our fortunes because of thy coming. We felt safe with one who had already travelled far and knew all about the outlandish ways of queer folks, blackamoors and these red men here. Now if so be thou art not to have a voice in the managing we be cheated and know not what may befall us. There be many of the others who think as we do, not only laborers such as we, but many of the gentlemen who have little faith in them as have been set in the high places. Now I say to thee, let us three go amongst them we knows as are friendly to thee and we will speak in secret with them and we will draw together to-morrow at one end of this island, and there we will all stay until they agree to make thee President. And if fightin' comes o' it why all the better. What sayst thou, Captain?"

Smith did not answer at once. The friendliness of these men touched him deeply just at the moment when he was smarting under the treatment accorded him. He knew they spoke truth; there were a number of the colonists who had shown themselves friendly to him and who would be willing to stand by him. Moreover, he felt within himself the power to use them, to make them follow his bidding as Wingfield could never succeed in doing. It was less for personal gratification he was tempted to consent than for the knowledge that his leadership would benefit the colony as would that of none of his fellow adventurers. He was not a vain man, but one conscious of unusual powers.

"If we were strong enough to gain and hold part of the stores and one of the vessels, would ye let me lead ye away to some other island of our own, men?" he asked, and immediately saw in his imagination the possibilities of such a step.

"Aye, aye. Captain," cried all three, "and we'd be strong enough too, never fear," added Hugh.

The temptation to John Smith was a strong one, and he walked up and down weighing the matter. What consideration after all did he owe to those who had not considered him? He had no fear of failure; he had come safely through too many dangers not to be confident. It was only the first step that he doubted. The men, he could see, were growing impatient, yet he did not speak. Suddenly an arrow whizzed close to his ear and fell at his feet.

"The savages!" cried Dickon.

Smith peered towards the woods beyond the water and imagined he could see half hidden behind a birch tree a naked figure.

"Let us go back and warn the Council," he said, turning towards the way he had come. "I scarcely think that they will attack us, particularly if we stay together."

He stood still a moment lost in thought. Then he said:

"That's the word, Dickon, *if we stay together*! Nay, frown not, Hugh. Put out of thy mind all that we have spoken of this last half-hour, as I shall put it out of mine. We must stand together, men, here in this new world. Ye three stand by me because we're all neighbors and Lincolnshire-born; but here in this wilderness we're all neighbors, English-born, just like a bigger shire. It's no time now when savages are about us all, to be thinking of our own little troubles. We must e'en forget them and stick together for the good of us all. Will ye promise, men?"

"Since 'tis so thou hast decided, Captain," answered Dickon.

"I'm for or against, as thou wilt," said Hugh, "but I'd been glad hadst thou chosen to fight instead o' to kiss."

And Hob, who had not spoken a word of his own invention up to now, spake solemnly:

"I'll not blab. Captain, how near thou wast to the fightin'."

When they got back to the site of the future Jamestown Smith, who had made up his mind to do what seemed to him right no matter what reception his advice received, told President Wingfield of the hidden bowman and warned him of the danger to those who might straggle away from their companions. But the members of the Council, whether they would be beholden to Smith not even for advice, or whether the friendly attitude of the Indians at first which was now just beginning to change, influenced them, refused to believe that the savages intended to molest them and refused to admit the necessity of putting up a palisade or taking other precautions against them.

Each day the work of clearing the ground and of setting up the tents proceeded apparently more rapidly than the day before, as the results were more visible. Every one was so wearied with the cramped life aboard ship for so many weeks that he was glad to stretch himself on the earth or on improvised beds. Smith, to give an example to some of the gentlemen who stood with folded arms looking on while the mechanics worked, swung axe and wielded hammer lustily. Yet he was very unhappy at the manner in which he was still treated and he eagerly seized an opportunity to leave the island.

With Captain Newport and twenty others, he set out in one of the ships' boats to explore the upper part of the river. They were absent a number of days, after having ascended the James as far as the great falls near the Powhata, a Powhatan village near the site of the present city of Richmond. Then they returned to Jamestown.

On their arrival they were greeted with the grave news that during their absence the Indians had killed a boy and wounded seventeen of the colonists. A shot fired from one of the ships had luckily so terrified the savages that they made off for the woods. Now the Council was forced to recognize the need of some protection and ordered every one to stop work on everything else until a strong palisade and a rough fort had been built.

It was now June. Suddenly, to the astonishment of all, the Indians approached and made signs that they desired to enter into amicable relations with the white men. They jumped out from their boats and fingered the clothes of the colonists, their guns and their food, showing great curiosity at everything. The next day, perhaps because the Council had seen the folly of their suspicions or had realized the value of Smith's military experience and knowledge, the state of his semi-imprisonment, which had lasted since the early part of the voyage, was put an end to. Now that all seemed peaceful, from without and within, as a sign of gratitude and of their brotherly feelings towards each other, all the colonists partook of the Communion together, kneeling in the temporary shed covered with a piece of sail-cloth which served as a church.

Then on the seventh of June they stood on the river bank, looking gravely, with many doubts and fears in their hearts, at the *Discovery* as she sailed for England, bearing Captain Newport away, and leaving them alone in Virginia.

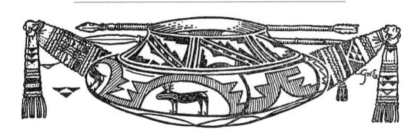

CHAPTER VII

A FIGHT IN THE SWAMP

Not a day passed without new rumors at Werowocomoco of the white strangers and their curious habits.

Pamunkeys from the tops of swaying trees on either bank watched eagerly the doings of the colonists, and runners bore the word of every movement to both Opechanchanough at Kecoughtan and to The Powhatan at his village. Curiosity and consternation were equally balanced in the minds of the red men. What meant this coming from the rising sun of beings whose ways no man could fathom? Were they gods enjoying a charmed life, against whom neither bow nor shaman's medicine might avail? About the council fires in every village this was debated. The old chiefs, wise in the traditions of their people, spake of prophecies which foretold the coming of heroes with faces pale as water at dawn who should teach to the tribes good medicine and bring plentiful harvests and rich hunting. Others recalled the vague rumors which had come from far, far away in the Southland, from tribes whose very names were unknown, of other palefaces (the Spanish colonists in the West Indies), who had brought fire and fighting into peaceful, happy islands of the summer seas, who like terrible, powerful demons, spread about them death and strange diseases.

Then came to the councils the comforting word of the death of a white boy slain by a Pamunkey arrow. So they were mortal after all, said the chiefs, and they smoked their pipes more placidly as they sat around the fire. Against gods man could not know what action was right; but since these were but men who could hunger and thirst and be wounded, it behooved them to plan what measures should be adopted against them.

Many of the chiefs urged immediate steps.

"It is easy," said one, "to pull up a young oak sapling, whereas who may uproot a full-grown tree?"

Nautauquas, son of Powhatan, was among the most eager for action. He had won for himself the name of a great brave and a mighty hunter though still so young. Many a scalp hung to the ridgepole of his lodge and many a bear and wildcat had he slain at great risk to his life. Now here was a new way to distinguish himself—to go forth against dangers he could not even foresee. What magic these pale-faced strangers used to protect themselves was unknown; therefore if he and his band should overcome them and wipe away all traces of their short stay, it would be a tale for winter firesides and a song for singers of brave deeds as long as his nation endured.

"Let me go, my father," he pleaded. "Thou, who thyself hast conquered thirty tribes, grudge not this fame to thy son."

"Wait!" was Powhatan's only answer.

The shamans and priests had advised the werowance thus. Not yet had they fathomed Okee's intentions in regard to these newcomers, though they had climbed to the top of the red sandy hills at Uttamussack where stood the three great holy lodges filled with images, and they had fasted and prayed that Okee would reveal to them what he desired. Powhatan, in spite of his years, felt the urge of action, and his heart leaped up when his favorite son gave voice to his own wishes. He longed to take the warpath, to glide through the forest, to spy upon the strangers who had dared make a place for themselves in his dominion, and then to fall upon them, terrifying them with his awful war-cry as he had terrified so many of his enemies. Yet he dared not do this yet: he was not only a great war chief, but a leader of his people in peace. Okee had not yet spoken. Perchance the men with strange faces and strange tongues would of their own accord acknowledge his sovereignty, and there might be no need of sacrificing against them the lives of his young men.

All this he was thinking when he bade Nautauquas wait; but there was no one who read his mind, yet no one who dared to disobey him.

When Nautauquas came out from his father's lodge he took his bow and quiver and went into the forest to hunt. In his disappointment he had a hatred of more words and a longing for deeds. He ran swiftly and had reached a spot where he felt sure that he would find a flock of wild turkeys, when he saw Pocahontas ahead of him. She too was hurrying, bent evidently on some errand that absorbed her, for she did not stop to peer up at the birds or to pull the flowers as she was wont to do.

"Matoaka," he called, "whither goest thou?"

"To see the strangers and their great white birds again which I beheld from Kecoughtan, Brother. I cannot rest for my eagerness to know what they are like nearby."

"Hast thou not heard our father's word that no one shall go near the island where the strangers be?" he asked.

"My father meaneth not me," she answered proudly. "As thou knowest, he permitteth me much that is forbidden to others."

"But not this, little Sister. Only just this moment did he forbid me to go thither. His mind is set thereon; tempt not his anger. Even though he loves thee well, if thou disobeyest his command in this matter he will deal harshly with thee. Turn back with me, Matoaka, and thou shalt help me shoot."

Pocahontas was reluctant to give up her long-planned expedition, but she let herself be persuaded. She remembered that Powhatan that very day had ordered one of his squaws beaten until she lay at death's door. Moreover, it was a great joy to hunt with Nautauquas and to see which of them would bring down the most turkeys. They were needed by the squaws who had been complaining that the braves were growing lazy and did not keep them supplied with meat.

While Powhatan's two children were adding to the well-filled larder of Werowocomoco, there was real dearth of food at Jamestown. The stores, many of them musty and almost inedible after the long voyage, were growing daily scarcer. There was fish in the river, but the colonists grew weary of keeping what they called "a Lenten diet," and in their dreams munched juicy sirloins of fat English beef. At first their nearby Indian neighbors had been glad to trade maize and venison for wonderful objects, dazzling and strange; but now, whether owing to word sent by Powhatan or for other reasons, they came no more with provisions to barter. John Smith, seeing that supplies were the first necessity of the colony, had gone forth on several expeditions up the different rivers in search of them. By bargaining, by cajolery, by force, he had managed each time to renew the storehouse. Yet again it was almost empty and starvation threatened.

Something must be done at once, and the Council sat in debate upon the serious matter. Captain John Smith waited until the others had had their say, and nothing practical had been suggested, then he rose and began:

"Gentlemen of the Council, there is but one thing to do. Since our larder will not fill itself, needs must someone go forth again to seek for food. Give me two men and one of the ship's boats and I will set off to the northward, up that river the Indians call the Chickahominy and, God helping me, I will bring back provisions for us all and make some permanent treaty with the savages to supply us till our crops be grown."

President Wingfield agreed to Smith's demand. The barge was got ready with a supply of beads and other glittering articles from Cheapside booths, and Smith set off with the good wishes of the wan-faced colonists.

After they had reached what seemed to Smith a likely spot for trading, he took two men, Robinson and Emery, and two friendly natives in a canoe and set off to explore the river further, bidding the others to wait for him where he left them and on no account to venture nearer shore.

He was glad to be away from the noise of complaining men at Jamestown, many of whom were ill and fretful from lack of proper nourishment and some, who because they were gentlemen, would not labor yet repined that they could not live as gentlefolk at home. On this expedition he was with friends, even though he knew not what enemies might be lurking on the shore; and he realized that the natives were growing less friendly as time went on and they began to lose their first awe of the white men. But he had no fear for himself; he had faced too many dangers in his adventurous life to conjure up those to come.

As they paddled up the Chickahominy the men began to talk of old days in England before they had dreamed of trying their fortunes in a new world, but Smith bade them be silent so that he could listen for the slightest sound to indicate the vicinity of a human habitation.

"Make friends as soon as thou canst with the copper men, Captain," whispered Robinson, "for I be main hungry and can scarce wait till thou hast bartered this rubbish 'gainst good victuals."

"Pull thy belt in a bit tighter, men," suggested the Captain grimly; "if I understand all they tell me, the Indians can beat the most devout Christians in fasting. 'Tis one virtue we may learn from them."

They kept in the middle of the stream to be safe from any arrows that might be shot at them from shore; but after many hours of this caution. Smith determined to explore a little on land. To his practiced eye a certain little inlet seemed so suitable a landing for canoes that he felt sure an Indian village could not be far off.

"Push out into the stream again," he commanded as he stepped ashore, "and wait for me there."

John Smith strode into the forest, ready for friendship or war, since he knew not the temper of the natives of that region. Suddenly, as he came out upon an open space where a morass stretched from a hill to the river, two hundred shrieking savages rushed upon him, shooting their arrows wildly at all angles.

"War then!" cried Smith aloud, and as one young brave in advance of the others stopped to take aim, he leaped forward and caught him. Ripping off his own belt. Smith bound the astonished Indian to his left arm so that he could use him as a living buckler. Thus protected, he fired his pistol and the ball, entering the breast of an older chief, killed him instantly. For a moment the strange fate which had overtaken their leader checked the onslaught, while his companions stooped down, one behind the other, to examine the wound made by the demon weapon. This respite gave Smith time to whip out his sword, and whirling it about him, he kept his enemies at a distance. He might have succeeded in defending himself thus for some time longer, for the savages had ceased to shoot, not certain whether their arrows would not be ineffectual upon an invulnerable body, but all at once he became aware of a new danger. The marshy ground on which he stood had softened with his weight and that of his living shield and he now felt himself sinking deeper and deeper into the morass until he was submerged up to his waist. Still the Indians, doubtless fearing he had some other strange weapons or evil medicines in his power, did not rush forward to attack him.

The day was bitterly cold, and the stagnant water struck a chill to his very bones. His teeth began to chatter with cold, not fright. It was almost with a sense of relief that he saw the Indians start towards him. Carefully treading in their light moccasined feet, they gradually surrounded him and two, taking hold of him, while others loosened the bound brave, they drew him up from the slushy earth by the arms.

He was now a captive, and not for the first time in his life. There was nothing to be gained, he knew, by struggling, and he faced them with no sign of fear. They led him to a fire which was blazing not far off on firmer ground where sat a chief, who, he learned, was the werowance Opechanchanough.

At a word of command from him, the guards moved aside and the huge warrior walked slowly around Smith, examining him from head to foot.

There was a pause which, the Englishman knew, might be broken by an order to torture and kill him. He did not understand their hesitancy, but he meant at any rate to take advantage of it. He must engage the attention of the giant chief before him. Slowly he pulled from his pocket his heavy silver watch and held it up to his own ear.

Never had Opechanchanough and his men experienced such an awe of the unknown. For all they could tell, this small ball in the white man's hand might contain a medicine more deadly than that of his pistol. They stood like children in a thunderstorm, not knowing when or where the bolt might strike.

But nothing terrible came to pass. Then Opechanchanough's curiosity was aroused and he put out his hand for the watch. Smith, smiling, held it towards him in his palm and then laid it against the chief's ear, saying in the Pamunkey tongue: "Listen." Opechanchanough jumped with astonishment and cried out:

"A spirit! A spirit! He hath a spirit imprisoned!"

Then one by one the captors crowded forward to look at the "turtle-of-metal-that-hath-a-spirit," and many were the exclamations of astonishment.

In order to increase this feeling of awe and to lengthen the delay, though he did not know what he could even hope to happen. Smith felt in his pocket again and brought out his travelling compass. It was of ivory and the quivering needle was pronounced by Opechanchanough to be another spirit.

But suddenly, without warning, two of the younger warriors, who had evidently determined once for all to discover if this stranger were vulnerable or not, seized Smith and dragging him swiftly to a tree, threw a cord of deer thong about him, drawing it fast. Then they notched their arrows and took aim at his heart. "In one second it will be over," thought Smith, "life, adventures, my ambitions and my troubles."

Then Opechanchanough called out to the braves, holding up the compass. Frowning with disappointment, the young men loosed their captive and Smith realized that it was again the chief's curiosity which had saved his life. By means of such Indian words as he knew and by the further aid of signs he endeavored to explain its usage.

"See," he said, pointing, "yon is the north whence comes popanow, the winter; and there behind us lies cohattayough, the summer. I turn thus and lo, the spirit in the needle loves the north and will not be kept from it."

When all had looked at the compass, Opechanchanough took it again in his hand, holding it gingerly as he would have held a papoose if a squaw had given one to his care. This was something precious and he meant to keep it, yet he did not know what it might do to him. At any rate, it would be a good thing to take with him the man who did understand it.

"Come," he said, "since thou canst understand our words, come and eat in the lodge of the Pamunkeys."

And Smith, ignorant of when death might fall upon him, followed. That day they feasted him, and the half-starved Englishman ate heartily for the first time since he set foot in the new world. At least he had gained strength now to bear bravely whatever might await him. The next day he was bidden accompany them, and they marched swiftly and steadily for many hours through the forest to Orapeeko. It may be that Opechanchanough's messengers had informed him mistakenly that Powhatan was at that village which, after Werowocomoco, he most frequented; but on their arrival there they found the lodges empty except the great treasure-house full of wampum, skins and pocone, the precious red paint used for painting the body. This was guarded by priests, and while Opechanchanough talked with them. Smith marvelled at the images of a dragon, a bear, a leopard and a giant in human form that ornamented the four corners of the treasure-house.

Evidently the priests were giving the werowance some advice. Smith wondered whether the savages offered human sacrifices to their Okee and if such were to be his fate. But the night was passed quietly there; the next day was spent in marching, and the following night in another village. Everywhere he was the object of the greatest interest: braves, squaws and children crowded about him, fingered his clothes, pulled at his beard and asked him questions. The Englishman observed them with the same interest. He noticed how the men wore but one garment leggings and moccasins made in one piece, and how they were painted in bright colors, many wearing symbols or rude representations of some animal which he learned was their "medicine." He watched the women as they embroidered and cooked, tanned hides and dyed skins, scolded and petted their children. Their lodges were lightly built, he saw, yet strong and well-suited for their occupants. Many of the young men and maidens made him think of deer in the swiftness of their movements and in the suppleness of their bodies.

After many days of travelling, in which Smith believed that they often retraced their steps, they found themselves one afternoon at the outskirts of a larger village than any they had yet entered. Dogs barked and children shouted as they neared the palisade, and men and women came running from every side.

"Certainly," thought Smith, "we are expected. Never in an English village have I seen a Savoyard with a trained bear make more excitement than doth here Captain John Smith."

CHAPTER VIII

POCAHONTAS DEFIES POWHATAN

"Princess, Pocahontas!" cried Claw-of-the-Eagle, as he pointed excitedly to the outskirts of the village, "look, yonder come thy uncle and his men bringing the white prisoner with them."

Pocahontas, who a few moments before had jumped down from the grapevine swing, where she had been idling, to peep into Claw-of-the-Eagle's pouch at the luck his hunting had brought him, now started off running after the son of old Wansutis, who was speeding towards the gathering crowd. Never in all her life had she desired anything as much as she now desired to gain a sight of this stranger.

"What doth he look like?" she called out, panting, to the boy ahead; but her own swiftness answered the question, for she was soon abreast of the procession. There, walking behind her uncle, unbound and apparently unconcerned, she beheld the white man. Her eyes devoured every detail of his appearance. She was almost disappointed to find that he had only one head and two eyes like all the rest of her world. But his beardedness, so unknown among her people, his youth, which showed itself more in his figure and in his step than in his weatherworn features, his cloth jerkin and his leather boots, but above all, the strange hue of his face and hands offered enough novelty to satisfy her.

Smith noticed the Indian maiden, already in her thirteenth year, tall above the average. In his wanderings through the Pamunkey villages he had seen many young girls and squaws, but none of them had seemed to him so well built or with such clean-cut features as this damsel who gazed at him so fixedly. When Opechanchanough, catching sight of her, made a gesture of recognition, Smith knew that she must have some special claim to distinction, since it was unusual, he had observed, for a chief to notice anyone about him while occupied in what might be called official duty. He felt sure too that he had now come to the end of his journeyings. In the other towns through which he had travelled he had heard men speak of Werowocomoco and of the great werowance who held sway there, the dreaded ruler over thirty tribes. This large village he knew must be the seat of the head of the Powhatan Confederacy and he was about to be led before him. What would happen then, he wondered, as he walked calmly through the crowd who eyed him curiously.

And this, too, was what Pocahontas was thinking: what would her father do with this man? Would his strange medicine, which those who had ventured to Jamestown had much discussed, assist him in his peril? She had listened to much talk lately about the necessity of getting rid of all the white faces who had dared come and build them houses on land which had belonged to her people since the beginning of the world. Here was the first chance her father had had to deal with the interlopers. She determined to see and hear all that should take place, so she hurried ahead to the ceremonial lodge, where she was sure to find her father, and entered it unchallenged by the guards.

Once inside, she realized that the stranger's coming had been expected; probably Opechanchanough had sent runners ahead whom she had not chanced to see. All the chiefs were gathered there waiting and there also sat the Queen of Appamatuck, the ruler of an allied tribe. She noticed that her father, in the centre of a raised platform at the other end of the lodge, had on his costliest robe of raccoon skin, the one she had embroidered for him. All the chiefs were painted, as were the squaws, their shoulders and faces streaked with the precious pocone red. She regretted that she had not had time to put on her new white buckskin skirt and her finest white bead necklace, since this was such a gala occasion. On the other side of Powhatan sat one of his squaws, and her brothers and her uncles Opitchapan and Catanaugh squatted directly before him. She herself stood against the wall nearest to the mother of her sister Cleopatra. She wished she had tried to bring in Claw-of-the-Eagle with her. How interested he would have been; but it was not likely that he would manage to get past the guards now, since there were so many of his elders who must be excluded for lack of room.

While she was still looking around to see who the lucky spectators were, the entrance to the lodge was darkened and a great shouting went up from all the braves as Opechanchanough strode in, followed by his prisoner.

Powhatan sat in silence until Smith stood directly before him, and then he spoke:

"We have waited many days and nights to behold thee, wayfarer from across the sea."

Smith, looking up at him, saw a finely built man of about sixty years, with grizzled hair and an air of command. He smiled to himself at the strangeness of his fancy's play, but the air of this savage chieftain, this inborn dignity of one conscious of his power, he had seen in but one other person—Good Queen Bess!

"I too have listened to many voices which have told of thy might, great chief," he answered, speaking the unfamiliar words slowly and distinctly.

Then in the pause that followed the Queen of Appamatuck came forward and held out to Smith a bowl of water for him to wash his hands in. Pocahontas leaned eagerly forward to see whether the water would not wash off some paint from his hands, leaving them the color of her own, for might it not be, she had questioned Claw-of-the-Eagle, that these strangers were only *painted* white? But even after Smith had wiped his fingers upon the turkey feathers the Queen handed to him, they remained the same tint as his face.

At the command of Nautauquas, the slaves began to bring in food for the feast which preceded any discussion of moment. An enemy, be he the bitterest of an individual or of the tribe, must never be denied hospitality. Baskets and gourds there were filled with sturgeon, turkey, venison, maize bread, berries and roots of various kinds, and earthern cups of pawcohiccora milk made from walnuts. Powhatan had motioned Smith to be seated on a mat beside the fire, and taking the first piece of venison, the werowance threw it into the flames as the customary sacrifice to Okee. Then he was served again, and after him each dish was offered to the prisoner.

There was little talk while the feasting continued. Pocahontas, who did not eat, lost no motion of the stranger's.

"At least," she thought, "he lives by food as we do." And she watched to see whether he would entangle his meat in his beard.

At last every one had eaten his fill and the dogs snarled and fought over the scraps until they were driven from the lodge. Then Powhatan began to question his prisoner.

"Art thou a king?"

"Nay, lord," replied the Englishman when he had comprehended the question; "I but serve one who ruleth over many thousand braves."

"Why didst thou leave him?"

Smith was about to answer that they sought new land to increase his sovereign's dominions, but he realized that this was not a favorable moment for such a statement.

"We set forth to humble the enemies of our king, the Spaniards," he replied, and in this he was not telling an untruth, because the colonization in Virginia had for one of its aims the destruction of Spanish settlements in the New World.

"And why did ye come ashore on my land and build yourselves lodges on my island?"

"Because we were weary of much buffeting by the waves and in need of fresh food."

For a moment at least Powhatan seemed content with this explanation. His curiosity in regard to the habits of these strangers was almost as keen as that of his daughter.

"Tell me of thy ways," he commanded. "Why dost thou wear such garments? Why hast thou hair upon thy mouth? Worship ye an Okee? How mighty are thy medicine-men? And how canst thou build such great canoes with wings?"

Smith endeavored to satisfy him. He dilated upon the power of King James, though in his mind that sovereign could not be compared for regal dignity to this savage; the bravery of the colonists, the wonder of silken garments and jewels worn by the men and women of his land. And remembering his duty as a Christian, he tried to explain the mysteries of the Christian faith to this heathen, but he found his vocabulary unequal to this demand. He could see that he was making an impression on his listeners; the greater their awe for his powers, the more chance that they might be afraid to injure him. Opechanchanough spoke to his brother, telling him of the watch and compass. Powhatan seized them eagerly, turned them over and over and held them to his ear, listening while Smith explained their use.

"I would fain know of those strange reeds ye carry that bear death within them," commanded the werowance again. "By what magic are ye served? Could not one of our shamans or our braves make it obey him also?"

"LET US BE FRIENDS AND ALLIES, OH POWHATAN"

Smith was aware that the Indians' fear of the white man's guns was the colony's greatest protection. So he answered:

"If my lord will come to Jamestown, as we call the island, since we know not by what name ye call it, he himself shall see guns as much greater than this one at my side," and he pointed to his pistol, "as thou art greater than lesser werowances."

This answer moved Powhatan strangely. He spoke rapidly, in words Smith could not understand, to some of the chiefs before him. Then turning to Smith again, and speaking in a tone no longer curious but cold and stern, he asked:

"How soon will ye set forth in your canoes again for your own land?"

The question Smith had dreaded must now be answered. There was danger in what he must say, yet perchance there was also the hope of soothing the fears of the savages. At all events, a lie were useless even if he had been able to tell one.

"The land is wide, oh mighty king, this land of thine, and a fair land with food enough and space aplenty for many tribes. Bethink thee of thine enemies who dwell to the north and west of thee who envy thy corn fields and thy hunting grounds. Will it not advantage thee when we, to whom thou wilt present, or perchance if it please thee better, *sell* a little island and a few fields on the mainland, shall join with thee and thy braves on the warpath against thy foes, and when we destroy them for thee with our guns? Let us be friends and allies, oh Powhatan. I will speak frankly, as it behooveth one to speak to a great chief, this land pleaseth us and we would gladly abide in it."

The Englishman could not read in the expressionless face of the werowance what he was thinking of this proposition—the first attempt of the colonists to explain their presence in the Indians' domain. But the shouting from all sides of the lodge which followed showed him that the other chiefs were strongly roused by his words. There was a long consultation: Powhatan spoke first, then a priest of many years who was listened to with great consideration, then one of the older squaws expressed her opinion, which seemed to voice that of the braves as well. Smith, knowing that his fate was being decided, tried to catch their meaning, but they spoke so rapidly that he comprehended only a phrase here and there. At last, however, Powhatan waved his hand for silence and issued a command.

It was the death sentence. Every eye was turned upon Smith. Well, they should see how an Englishman met death. He smiled as if they had brought him good news. If only his death could save the colony, it had been indeed a welcome message. Not that he did not love life, but he was one of those souls to whom an ambition, a cause, a quest, is dearer than life. And because of its very weakness, its dependence upon him, the colony had come to be like a child he must protect.

Pocahontas, when she listened to her father's verdict, felt within her heart the same queer faintness she had experienced when Claw-of-the-Eagle was running the gauntlet. And seeing the Englishman smile, she knew him to be a brave man, and somehow felt sorry for him. She was sorry for herself also. He could have told her many new tales of lands and people, far more interesting that those of Michabo, the Great Hare. How eagerly she would have listened to him! Her father was a wise leader and he did well to fear, as she had heard him tell his chiefs, the presence in his land of these white men with their wonderful medicine; but why must he kill this leader of them, why not keep him always a prisoner?

She saw that the slaves had lost no time in obeying the command given them—they were dragging in the two great stones that had not been used for many moons. These were set in the open space before Powhatan and she knew exactly what was to follow.

Was there any possible way of escape? John Smith asked himself. If there had been but one loading in his pistol he would have fired at the werowance and trusted to the confusion to rush through the crowd and out of the lodge. But it was empty. No use struggling, he thought; he had seen men who met death thus discourteously and he was not minded to be one of them. So, when at a quick word from Powhatan two young braves seized him, he made no resistance. They threw him down on the ground, then lifted his head up on the stones, while another savage, a stone hatchet in his hand, strode forward and took his stand beside him.

"Well," thought John Smith, "life is over; I have travelled many a mile to come to this end. What will befall Jamestown? At least I didn't fail them. I'm glad of that now."

He saw Powhatan lean forward and give a sign; then the red-painted face of his executioner leered at him and he watched the tomahawk descending and instinctively closed his eyes.

But it did *not* descend. After what seemed an hour of suspense he opened his eyes again to see why it delayed. The man who held it still poised in the air was gazing impatiently towards the werowance, at whose feet knelt the young girl Smith had noticed by the palisade. The child was pleading for his life, he could see that. Were these savages then acquainted with pity, and what cause had she to feel it for him?

But the werowance would not listen to her pleadings and ordered her angrily away. His voice was terrifying and the other squaws, fearing his rage might be vented on the child, tried to pull her up to the seat beside them. Powhatan nodded to the executioner to obey his command.

With a bound Pocahontas flung herself down across Smith's body, got his head in her arms and laid down her own head against his. The tomahawk had stopped but a feather's breadth from her black hair, so close that the Indian who held it could scarcely breathe for fear it might have injured the daughter of The Powhatan.

For a moment it seemed to all the anxious onlookers as if the werowance, furious at such disobedience, were about to order the blow to fall upon both heads. There was silence, and those at the back of the lodge crowded forward in order not to miss what was to come. Then Powhatan spoke:

"Rise, Matoaka! and dare not to interfere with my justice!"

"Nay, father," cried Pocahontas, lifting her head while her arms still lay protectingly about Smith's neck, "I claim this man from thee. Even as Wansutis did adopt Claw-of-the-Eagle, so will I adopt this paleface into our tribe."

Every one began to talk at once: "She desires a vain thing!"—"She hath the right."—"If he live how shall we be safe?"—"Since first our forefathers dwelt in this land hath this been permitted to our women!"

Powhatan spoke sternly:

"Dost thou claim him in earnestness, Matoaka?"

"Aye, my father. I claim him. Slay him not. Let him live amongst us and he shall make thee hatchets, and bells and beads and copper things shall he fashion for me. See, by this robe I wrought to remind thee of thy love for me, I ask this of thee."

"So be it," answered The Powhatan.

Pocahontas rose to her feet and, taking Smith by the hand, raised him up, dazed at his sudden deliverance and not understanding how it had come about.

CHAPTER IX

SMITH'S GAOLER

The following morning Claw-of-the-Eagle, passing before the lodge assigned to the prisoner, beheld Pocahontas seated on the ground in front of it.

"What dost thou here?" he asked, "and where be the guards?"

"I sent them off to sleep as soon as the Sun came back to us," she answered, looking up at the tall youth beside her. "I can take care of him myself during the day."

"Hast thou seen him yet? Tell me what is he like. I saw him but for the minute yesterday."

"He sleeps still. I peeped between the openings of the bark covering here and beheld him lying there with all those queer garments. I am eager for his awakening; there are so many questions I would ask him."

"Let me have a look, too," pleaded the boy.

Pocahontas nodded and motioned graciously to the opening of the lodge. It pleased her to grant favors, and Powhatan sometimes smiled when he marked how like his own manner of bestowing them was that of his daughter.

With the same caution with which he crept after a deer in a thicket, Claw-of-the-Eagle moved on hands and knees along the ground within the lodge. Lying flat on his stomach, he gazed at the Englishman. He had heard repeated about the village the night before the details of his rescue as they had taken place within the ceremonial wigwam. Those who told him were divided in their opinions; some looked upon Powhatan's decision as a danger to them all, and others scouted the idea that those palefaces were to be feared by warriors such as the Powhatans. Claw-of-the-Eagle, however, did not waver in his belief: each of the white strangers should be killed off as quickly as might be. His loyalty to his adopted tribe was as great as if his forefathers had sat about its council fires always. He was sorry that Pocahontas, much as she pleased him, had persuaded her father to save the life of the first of the palefaces that had fallen into his power. He believed The Powhatan himself now regretted that he had yielded to affection and to an ancient custom, and that he would gladly see his enemy dead, in order that the news carried to his interloping countrymen might serve as a warning of the fate that awaited them all.

Suppose then—the thought flashed through his brain—that he, Claw-of-the-Eagle, should make this wish a fact! Powhatan would never punish the doer of the deed.

He crept nearer still to the sleeping man, loosening the knife in his girdle. There was no sound within the lodge, only the faint crooning of Pocahontas without; yet something, some feeling of danger, aroused the Englishman. Through his half-closed lids he scarce distinguished the slowly advancing red body from the red earth over which it was moving. But when the boy was close enough to touch him with the outstretched hand. Smith opened his eyes wide. He did not move, did not cry out, though he saw the knife in the long thin fingers; all he did was to fix his gaze sternly upon the boy's face. Claw-of-the-Eagle tried to strike, but with those fearless eyes upon him he could not move his arm.

Slowly, as he had come, he crawled back to the entrance, unable to turn his head from the man who watched him. It was only when he was out in the air again that he felt he could take a long breath.

"He is a good sleeper," was all he remarked.

"And doubtless he is as good an eater and will be hungry when he wakes. Wilt thou not stop at our lodge, Claw-of-the-Eagle, and bid them bring me food for him?"

He did as she asked, and shortly after the squaws arrived with earthen dishes filled with bread and meat. They peered eagerly through the crevices till Pocahontas commanded them to be off. Hearing a noise within the lodge, she was about to bear the food inside when Smith stepped to the entrance.

He was astonished to see the kind of sentinel they had set to guard him. He had expected to find that his unexpected guest would be waiting outside for another chance at his life, and he preferred to hasten the moment. He realized that this maiden, however, would be as efficient a gaoler as a score of braves. Should he dream of escaping, of finding his way without guides or even his compass, back to Jamestown, her outcry would bring the entire village to her aid. He recognized his saviour of the day before and bowed low, a bow meant for the princess and for his protector. Pocahontas, though a European salutation was as strange to her as Indian ways were to him, felt sure his ceremonious manner was intended to do her honor, and received it gravely and graciously.

"Here is food for thee, White Chief," she said, placing it on a mat she had spread on the ground; "sit and eat."

"It is welcome," he answered, "yet first harken to me. I have not words of thy tongue, little Princess, to pay thee for thy great gift, and though my words were as plentiful as the grains of sand by the waters, they were still too few to offer thee."

"Gifts made to chiefs," she answered with a dignity copied from her father's, "can never pay for princely benefits."

Smith could not help smiling at the grandiloquence of the child's language, for in spite of her height, he realized that her years were but few.

"Yet," she continued, seating herself, "it pleaseth me to receive thy thanks."

Now she put aside her grown-up air and her curious glances were those of the child she was. She fingered gently the sleeve of his doublet stained by the morass in which he had been captured and torn by the briars of the forests through which he had been led.

"'Tis good English cloth," he remarked, "to have withstood such storm, and I bless the sheep on whose backs it grew."

"What beasts are those?" she queried, and Smith endeavored to explain the various uses and the looks of Southdown flocks.

"Did thy squaws make thy coat for thee when thou hadst slain that—that new beast?"

"I have no squaw, little Princess."

"I am glad," she sighed.

"And why?"

"I do not know", her brow wrinkling as she tried to fathom her own feelings. "Perhaps it is because now thou wilt not pine for her and to be gone from amongst us."

"But I must leave here soon, little maid; my people at Jamestown are waiting for me."

He said this in order to try and discern what was the intention of Powhatan towards him. Now that his life was saved, his thought was for his liberty.

"Thou shalt not go," she cried, springing up. "Thou belongest to me and it is my will to keep thee that thou mayst tell me tales of the world beyond the sunrise and make new medicine for us. Thou shalt not go."

"So be it," said Smith in a tone he tried to render as unemotional as possible. He sighed inwardly as he thought of his fellows at Jamestown, ill, starving, and now doubtless believing him dead. Perhaps if he bided his time he would find some way of communicating with them. In the meantime, policy, as well as inclination, urged his making friends with this eager little savage maiden.

Now that he did not attempt to oppose her, Pocahontas sank down again beside him. Already there was an audience: braves, squaws and children were crowding about, watching the paleface eat. Smith had learned since his captivity the value the Indians set upon an impassive manner, so he continued cutting off bits of venison and chewing them with as little attention to those about him as King James himself might show when he dined in state alone at Guildhall. But for Pocahontas's presence, whose claim to the captive every one respected, they would have come even nearer. As it was, one boy slipped behind her and jerked at Smith's beard. Pocahontas ordered him away and said in excuse:

"Do not be angry, he wanted only to find out if it were fast."

She shared the child's curiosity in regard to the beard. Might it not be, she wondered, some kind of adornment put on when he set out on the warpath, as her people decked themselves on special occasions with painted masks?

Smith tugged at his beard with both hands, smiling, and his audience burst out laughing. They could appreciate a joke, it seemed, and he was glad to see that their temper to him was friendly, for the moment at least. One of the older men pointed to the pocket in his jerkin and asked what he had in it. Compass and watch were gone, but Smith delved into its depths in hopes of finding something he had forgotten which might interest them. He brought out a pencil and a small note-book. He wrote a few words and handed them to Pocahontas, saying:

"These are medicine marks. If one should carry them to Jamestown they would speak to my people there and they would hear what I say at Werowocomoco."

Pocahontas shook her head as did those to whom she passed the leaf. The stranger might do many wonderful things, but this claim passed the bounds of even the greatest shaman's power.

Smith, however, determined to keep her thinking of the possibility of his return to Jamestown, continued:

"It is possible for me, in truth. Princess, and if thou would'st accompany me thither I could show thee stranger marvels still."

"Nay," she cried angrily, "thou shalt never go there. Thou art mine to do as I will. Is it not so?" she appealed to those about her.

They all shouted affirmation, confirming Smith's belief that his fate had been placed in a girl's hands. It was not the first time such a thing had happened to him; once before in his life a woman had been his gaoler, and he again made up his mind to bide his time. He answered the numerous questions put to him as best he could, about the number of days he had been with the Pamunkeys, his capture, and why he had separated from his fellows. In turn he questioned them about their harvests, the time and method of planting and the moon of the ripening of the maize; but the Indians showed plainly that they liked better to ask than to answer.

As the day advanced the crowd began to dwindle. The captive would not fail to be there whenever they desired to observe him and there was hunting to be done and cooking, and already some of the boys had strolled off to play their ever-fascinating game of tossing plumstones into the air. At last only Pocahontas was left with the prisoner.

Smith glanced about to see what the chances of escape might be should he make a sudden dash, but the sight of some braves at a lodge not more than a hundred feet away busied in sharpening arrowheads made him settle down again.

"Tell me, White Chief," said Pocahontas as she lighted a pipe she had filled with tobacco and gave it now to Smith, "tell me about thyself and thy people. Are ye in truth like unto us; do ye die as we do or can your medicine preserve you forever like Okee? Canst thou change thyself into an animal at will? If so, I fain would know how to do it, too."

Smith looked critically at the girl who sat on a mat beside him. He had never seen a maiden whose spirit was more eager for life. In her avidity for the miraculous he recognized something akin to his own love of adventure and desire to explore new lands and to sample new ways. She could not sail across the ocean in search of them as he had done—*he* was her great adventure, he realized, a personified book of strange tales to fire her imagination, as his had been stirred as a boy by stories of the kingdom of Prester John, of the El Dorado, of the Spanish Main and of the lost Raleigh Colony. The tobacco, which he had learned to smoke while with the Pamunkeys, soothed him; he was in no immediate danger; the warm sun was pleasant and the bright-eyed girl beside him was a sympathetic audience. He was always fond of talking, of living over the picturesque happenings that had crowded his twenty-eight years, and now he let himself run on, seeing again in his mind's eye the faces and the scenes of many lands, none of them, however, more strange than his present surroundings. The only difficulty was his insufficient vocabulary; but his mind was a quick and retentive one and each new word, once captured, came at his bidding.

Also, Pocahontas was a bright listener; she guessed at much he could not express and helped him with gesture and phrase.

"Princess," he began, when she interrupted:

"Call me Pocahontas as do my people. Perchance some day I'll tell thee my other name."

"Pocahontas, then," he repeated slowly, impressing the name on his memory, "I will obey thee. We are but men, as are thy kinsfolk, subject to cold and hunger, ills and death. Yet, as God, our Okee, is greater than your Okee, so our power and our medicine excel those of the mighty Powhatan and of his shamans. Thou asketh for tales of the land whence I come. They are so many that like the leaves of the forest I cannot count them. If we sat here until thou wert a wrinkled old crone like her yonder," and he pointed to old Wansutis who was hobbling by, "I could not relate half of them. Therefore, if it pleaseth thee, I will tell thee of some matters that have affected thy captive."

Pocahontas nodded her approbation.

"Our land, fair England, set in a stormy sea, is a mighty kingdom many, many days' journey over the waters. There all men and women are as white or whiter than I, now so weatherworn, as indeed are those of many other kingdoms further towards the sunrise. Our land, now ruled by a king who wields dominion over hundreds of tribes, was a few years ago under the sway of a mighty princess."

"Was she fair?" asked Pocahontas.

Smith hesitated. The glamour which had once hovered about "Good Queen Bess," obscuring the eyes of her loyal subjects, had since her death been somewhat dispelled. He thought of the pinched face, the sandy hair, the long nose, the small eyes—but then he had a vision of her as his boyish eyes had first beheld her, the sovereign riding her white steed before the host assembled to encounter the forces of the Armada Spain was sending to crush her realm.

"Not beautiful was she," he replied, "but a very king of men!"

He puffed a moment reminiscently, then continued:

"I was born some years ago in a part of our island called Lincolnshire, where it is low and marshy in places like unto the morass where thine uncle took me prisoner. Yet it is a land I love, though it grew too small for me, and when I was old enough to be a brave my hands itched to be fighting our enemies. So I went forth on the warpath against our foes in France and in the Netherlands. Then when I had fought for many moons and had gained fame as a warrior I felt a longing to return to mine own home. I abode there for a time, then I set forth once more and travelled long in a land called Italy and entered later the service of a great werowance, the Emperor Rudolph, to fight for him against the tribes of his foes, the Turks. I cannot explain to thee, Princess, how different are their ways from our ways; perchance theirs were nearer to thine understanding since they are not given to mercy and take to themselves many squaws; but let that rest. I fought them hard and often, and one day before the two armies, that ceased their combat to witness, I slew three of their great fighters, for which the Emperor did allow me to bear arms containing Three Turks' Heads—that is, as if one of thy kinsmen should sew upon his robe three scalps of enemies he had killed. But soon after that was I taken prisoner by these Turks and sold into captivity as a slave."

"Ah!" breathed Pocahontas deeply. For once in her life she was getting her fill of adventures.

"I was given as a slave to another princess—Tragabizzanda—in the City of Constantinople; then I was sent to Tartary, where I was most cruelly used. One day I fell upon the Bashaw of Nolbrits, who ill-treated me, and I slew him. I clothed myself in his garments and escaped into the desert and finally after many strange adventures I reached again a land where I had friends. Then—"

"Tell me of the princess," interrupted Pocahontas. "Did she ill-use thee also?"

"Nay, in truth, she was all kindness to me," replied Smith, his eye kindling at the remembrance of the Turkish lady who had aided him. "She was very beautiful, with lovely garments and rich jewels," he added, thinking to interest the girl with descriptions of her finery, "and I owe her many thanks."

"Was she more beautiful than I?" asked Pocahontas, her brows knitting angrily.

"She was very different," the amused Englishman answered. It was scarcely possible for him to consider these savages as being real human creatures, to be compared even with the Turks; yet he did not wish to hurt the feelings of one who had done so much for him. "She was a grown woman," he added, "and therefore it boots not to compare her with the child thou art."

"I am no child. I am a woman!" cried Pocahontas, springing up in a fury and rushed off like a whirlwind towards the forest.

John Smith looked after her in dismay. If he had turned his only friend against him then was he indeed in a sad plight!

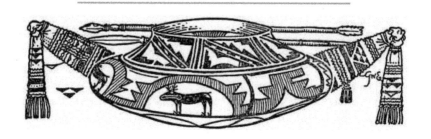

CHAPTER X

THE LODGE IN THE WOODS

Neither the rest of that day nor the next had Smith any speech with Pocahontas. True it was that she came accompanied by squaws and children, all eager to serve as cupbearers in order to observe the paleface closely. But she put down the food beside him and did not linger.

By the middle of the second day Smith found himself less an object of interest. Everyone in Werowocomoco had been to gaze at him and the older chiefs had sat and talked with him; but the Englishman could not discover what their opinion in regard to his coming or his future might be. Now there seemed to be something afoot which was engaging the attention of the braves who congregated together before the long lodge. Had it anything to do with his own fate, the captive wondered. The children, too, had found other things to interest them. He saw them, their little red bodies glistening in the sun, playing with the dogs or pretending they were a war party creeping through a hostile country. Smith missed them peering about the opening of his lodge, half amused, half frightened, when he attempted to make friends.

He leaned idly against the side of the wigwam, watching two squaws not far away who were tanning a deerskin and cutting it in strips for thread. Would the time ever come again, he wondered, when he would behold a white woman sewing or spinning?

He saw Pocahontas leave her lodge, but instead of coming in his direction, she ran towards the wigwams that skirted the forest and was soon out of sight. He could not see that a young Indian boy, astounded to catch sight of her in that unaccustomed part of the village, went to meet her.

"Is Wansutis by her hearth?" asked Pocahontas.

"She is," Claw-of-the-Eagle replied, and walked on beside her with no further word.

Pocahontas's heart was beating a little faster than usual. Wansutis still excited a feeling of awe and discomfort in the courageous child; she could not help experiencing a sort of terror when in her presence. Nevertheless she had now come of her own accord to ask the old woman for aid.

Claw-of-the-Eagle, though he would have bitten his tongue off rather than acknowledge his curiosity, was most eager to learn what had brought the daughter of Powhatan to his adopted mother's lodge. He entered it with

Pocahontas and pretended to be busying himself with stringing his bows in order to have an excuse for staying.

"Wansutis," began Pocahontas, standing in the sunshine of the entrance, to the old woman who sat smoking in the darkest part of the lodge, "thou hast the knowledge of all the herbs of the fields and of the forests, those that harm and those that help. Is it not so?"

The wrinkled squaw looked up, a drawn smile upon her lips, and said:

"And so Princess Pocahontas comes to old Wansutis for a love potion."

"Nay," cried the girl angrily, coming closer, "not so; I desire of thee something quite different—herbs that will make a man forget."

"The same herb for both," snapped the squaw; "for whom wilt thou brew it, for thine adopted son, thou who art no squaw and too young to have a son? I have no such herb, maiden, and if I had, thinkest thou I had not given it to Claw-of-the-Eagle to drink. Speak to her, son, and tell her if a man ever forgets."

Pocahontas turned a questioning glance on him and the young brave answered it:

"My thoughts are great and speedy travellers, Pocahontas; they take long journeys backwards to my father's and mother's people. They wander among old trails in the forests and they meet old friends by the side of burned-out campfires. Yet, when like weary hunters who have been seeking game all day, they return at night to their lodge, so mine return in gratitude to Wansutis. For she hath not sought to hinder them from travelling old trails, even as she hath not bound my feet to her lodge pole to keep them from straying."

"And if she had not left thee free," queried Pocahontas, "what wouldst thou have done?" Somehow, captivity and the thought of captives had suddenly become of extreme interest to the girl.

"I know not, Princess," answered the boy after pondering a moment, "yet had not my father and mother been dead I feel certain I should have sought to escape to them, even had thy father set all his guards about the village. But they were no more, and our wigwam afar off was empty; and so my heart finds rest in a new home and I gladly obey a new mother."

"Is it then so hard to forget an old lodge and other ways?" pondered the girl. "It seems to me that each day among strangers would be the beginning of a new life, that it would be pleasant to know I could not foresee what would come to pass before nightfall. Why," she queried, looking eagerly at both the old woman and the boy, "why should this paleface desire to return to the island where they sicken and starve while here he hath food in plenty?"

"Wait till thou thyself art among strangers away from thine own people," cried Wansutis sternly, and then she turned her back upon the young people and began to mutter.

"So thou hast no drink of forgetfulness to give me?" asked Pocahontas, hesitating at the entrance, to which she had retreated; but the old woman did not answer; and Pocahontas walked off slowly, meditating as she went, while Claw-of-the-Eagle, bow in hand, gazed after her.

It had grown dark and John Smith, his legs cramped with long sitting, stretched himself out by the side of the fire in his lodge into which he had thrown some twigs, so that the embers which had smouldered all day now blazed up brightly. The cheerful crackling was welcome, it seemed to him to speak in English words of home and comfort, not the heathenish jargon he had listened to perforce for several weeks. Not only was it a companion but a protection. While it blazed he might be seized and put to death, but at least he should see his enemies. He missed Pocahontas for her own sake, not only because her staying away argued ill for his safety. Gratitude was not the only reason for his interest in her: she seemed to him the freest, brightest creature he had ever come across, as much a part of the wilderness nature as a squirrel or a bird. Like all cultured Englishmen of his day, he had read many books and poems about shepherdesses in Arcadia and princesses of enchanted realms; but never yet had any writer, not even the great Spenser or Sir Philip Sidney, imagined in their words so free and wild and sylvan a creature as this interesting Indian maiden.

His thoughts were disturbed by the entrance of two Indians. "We are come," they said, "at The Powhatan's bidding to take thee to his lodge in the wood."

He knew not what this order might mean, yet he was glad that come what would, the monotony of his captivity was broken. He rose quickly and followed them through the village, each lodge of which had its ghostly curl of smoke ascending through the centre towards the dark sky. Within some of the wigwams he could see the fire and sitting around it families eating before lying down to sleep. Then they left the palisades of Werowocomoco behind them and came out into the forest, to a lodge as large as that in which he had first been led before Powhatan.

This one, however, was differently arranged. It was divided into two parts, separated by dark hanging mats that permitted no light to pass through. Into the smaller apartment, to give it such a name, Smith was ushered, and there the two Indians, after stirring up the fire and throwing on fresh logs, left him alone.

Not long, however, did Smith imagine himself the lodge's only inhabitant. The sound of muffled feet, even though they moved softly, betrayed the presence of a number of persons on the other side of the mat. His ears, his only sentinels, reported that the unseen foes had seated themselves and then, after a short silence, he heard a voice begin a low, weird chant. He could not understand the words, but from the monotonous shaking of a rattle and the steps that seemed to be moving in some dance round and round from one part of the room to the other, Smith was certain that it was a shaman beginning the chant for some sacred ceremony. Then one by one the different voices joined in, uttering hideous shrieks, and the ground shook with the shuffling of many feet. The sounds were enough to terrify the stoutest heart, and Smith had no doubt but that their song was a rejoicing over his coming death. Perhaps Powhatan, he thought, had only pretended to grant his daughter's request, having planned all along to put an end to him, and when the boy, who had doubtless been sent by him, had not succeeded, he had probably determined to kill him here. Or perhaps Pocahontas, now in anger with him, had withdrawn her claims to his life and left him to her father's vengeance.

The noise grew louder and more fiendish in character and the Englishman saw the corner of the mat begin to wave, to bulge as if a man were butting his head against it to raise it. Then he saw it lifted and in came a creature more hideous than Smith ever dreamed could exist. Painted all in red pocone, with breast tattooed in black, wearing no garment save a breech-clout and a gigantic headdress of feathers, shells and beads, he straightened himself to his great height. A horrible mask, distorting human lineaments, covered the face, and a medicine-bag of otter skin hung from his back and dangling from one arm as an ornament hung the dried hand of an enemy long since dead. On account of his stature and in spite of the mask, Smith recognized The Powhatan, and drew himself up proudly to meet his fate.

Behind their werowance now swarmed the other braves and chieftains, two hundred in all, and all with masks that made them as fearful, thought John Smith, as a troop of devils from hell.

To his astonishment, they did not fall upon him and in their shrieking he thought he could even distinguish the word "friend." The Powhatan alone of them all approached him, saying:

"Have no fear, my son; we are not come to harm thee. The ceremony which thou hast heard was to call Okee to witness to the friendship we have sworn thee. Henceforth are we and thou as of one tribe. No longer art thou a prisoner but free to come and go as thy brothers here, aye, even to return to thy comrades on the island if thou so desirest. When thou hast arrived there send unto me two of those great guns that spit forth fire and death that my name may become a still greater terror to mine enemies, and send to me also a grindstone such as thou hast told me of, that my squaws may use it for crushing maize. I ask not these gifts for naught. A great chief giveth ever gifts in return. Therefore I present to thee for thine own the land called Capahosick, where thou mayst live and build thee a lodge and take a squaw to till thy fields for thee. Moreover, I, The Powhatan, I, Wahunsunakuk, will esteem thee as mine own son from this day forth."

It was difficult for Smith during this discourse not to betray his astonishment. First came the relief at learning that he was not to be killed immediately and then the wonderful news that he was free to go to Jamestown. And if The Powhatan and his people had sworn friendship to him, would that not mean that through him the colony should be saved? He longed to know what had brought about this sudden change in his fate, but he could not ask. In as stately a manner as that of the werowance—so at variance with his appearance—and with the best words at his command, he spoke his thanks.

"I thank thee, great Powhatan, for thy words of kindness and the good news thou bringest me. In truth if thou wilt be to me a father, I will be to thee a son, and there shall be peace between Werowocomoco and Jamestown. If thou wilt send men with me to show me the way they shall return with presents for thee."

Powhatan gave certain orders and twelve men stepped forward and laid aside their sacrificial masks and announced themselves ready to accompany the paleface. Smith had not imagined that he could leave that night, but he was so eager to be off that he lost no time in his farewells.

They set forth into the forest which at first was not dense, and along its edge were clearings where the summer's maize had grown. Then the trees grew closer together, and to Smith there appeared no path between them, but his guides strode quickly along with no hesitation, though the night was a dark one. Six of the Indians went in front of him and six behind. There was no talking, only the faint sound from the Englishman's boots and his stumbling against trunks or rocks broke the silence. There was little chance of an enemy's coming so near to the camp of The Powhatan, nevertheless the Indians observed the usual caution.

To John Smith there was something ghostly about this excursion by night, through an unknown country, with unknown men. He could not help wondering whether he had understood correctly all that Powhatan had said, or whether he dared believe he had meant what he said, or if he had not planned to kill him in the wilderness away from any voice to speak in his favor. Even though the werowance himself were acting in good faith, might not others of the chiefs have plotted to put an end to the white man whose coming and whose staying were so beyond their fathoming? In spite of these thoughts he went on apparently as unconcernedly as though he were strolling along the king's highway near his Lincolnshire home.

The call of some animal, a wildcat perhaps, brought the little company to a hurried standstill, and a whispered consultation. The sound might really come from some beast, Smith knew; on the other hand, it might be either a signal made by foes of the Powhatans or the call of another party of their tribe about to join them. In the latter case it boded ill for him. He clasped a stone knife he had managed to secrete at Werowocomoco. He could not overhear what the Indians were saying, but they were evidently arguing. Then when they seemed to have come to some decision, they started on once more.

Though the forest was so sombre. Smith's eyes had grown more accustomed to the blackness and he began to distinguish between the various shades of darkness. Once or twice he thought he saw to the side of them another figure, moving or halting as they halted, but when he looked fixedly he could distinguish nothing but the trunk of some great tree.

On and on they went, mocked at by owls and whippoorwills, crossing streams over log bridges, wading through others when the cold water splashed at a misstep up in his face. At last the blackness turned to grey, in which he could make out the fingers of his hand. Dawn was near. Why, thought the Englishman, did they delay striking so long? If they meant to kill him, he hoped it might be done quickly. The phantom figure which had accompanied them after the halt following the wildcat call must soon act. Even a brave man must wish such a night as this to end.

Then the world ahead of him seemed to grow wider and lighter. The trees had larger spaces between them and the figures of the Indians were like a blurred drawing. Was it a star shining before them, that light that grew brighter and brighter?

"Jamestown!" he cried out in his own tongue. "Jamestown! Yon is Jamestown! God be praised!"

The Indians gathered about him and began to question him eagerly. Would he give presents to them all; would they have the guns to carry back with them?

As they stood in a little knot, each individual of which was growing more distinct, a young man ran up behind them.

"Claw-of-the-Eagle!" they exclaimed.

The boy put into the hands of the astonished Smith a necklace of white shells he remembered to have seen Pocahontas wear.

"Princess Pocahontas sends greetings," he said, "and bids thee farewell for to-day now that she hath seen thee safe again among thy people." His own scowl belied the kindliness of the message.

So John Smith knew that Pocahontas had accompanied him through the forest and that if death had been near him that night, it was she who had averted it from him.

CHAPTER XI

POCAHONTAS VISITS JAMESTOWN

"We have brought the white werowance safely back to his tribe again," said Copotone, one of the guides, as they approached the causeway leading to Jamestown Island.

"Of a surety," remarked Smith, "since thus it was that Powhatan commanded."

It was his policy—a policy which did credit to the head of one who, in spite of his knowledge of the world, was still so young—never to show any suspicion of Indian good-faith.

"Now that we have led thee thither," continued Copotone, who on his side had no intention of betraying any secrets of the past night, "wilt thou not fulfil thy promise and give to us the guns and grindstone?"

"Ye shall take to your master whatever ye can carry," answered Smith, whose heart was beating fast at the sight of the huts and fort before him, the outlines of which grew more distinct each moment with the brightening day. He had answered the hail of the sentry who, when he had convinced himself that his ears and eyes did not betray him, ran out and clasped the hands of one he had never thought to behold alive again.

"Captain!" he exclaimed, "but it is indeed a happy day that bringeth thee back to us, not but that some of them yonder," and he pointed significantly towards the government house, "will think otherwise."

The Indians in the meantime were looking about them with eager curiosity as they strode through the palisades into the fort. It was but a poor affair, judged by European military standards, and absolutely worthless if it should have to withstand a siege by artillery. But to the savages it was an imposing fortress, the very laws of its construction unknown to them, even the mortar between the logs, a substance of which they had no comprehension. Over the bastion as they emerged on the other side they beheld the English flag floating. This they took to be some kind of an Okee, in which opinion Smith's action confirmed them, for taking off his hat, he waved it in delight towards the symbol of all that was now doubly dear to him.

But it was the guns which claimed the chief attention of the savage visitors. There were four of them, all pointing towards the forest, iron culverins with the Tudor Rose and E.R. (Elizabeth Regina) moulded above their breeches.

"Are these the fire-tubes of which we have heard?" asked Copotone eagerly, longing to feel them, but not daring for fear of unknown magic.

"Aye," answered Smith, "art thou strong enough to carry one to Werowocomoco?"

The Indians looked them over appraisingly, wondering if they could drag them through the forest.

"Set the match to this one, Dickon," commanded Smith with a grim smile. "It behooves us to frighten well this escort of mine, or they would be trying to carry off one of my iron pets here to a strange kennel."

Dickon took up a tinder-box that lay on the bench beside him, and in a moment under the fixed gaze of his audience struck a light and applied it to the flax at the breech. There was a flash, then a loud report, and the Indians, as if actually hit, fell to the ground, where they stayed until they gradually convinced themselves that they were unhurt.

"If ye had been in front instead of behind ye had been killed," Smith said solemnly, desiring to impress them with the terrors of the white man's magic.

The Indians got to their feet and, though they said nothing, and did not attempt to run, John Smith knew that they were more terrified than they had ever been in their lives.

"Come," he said, leading the way from the fort to the town. "Since ye find our guns too heavy and too noisy I will seek more suitable presents for Powhatan and for you."

The colonists, roused by the cannon shot, had run out from their doors to see what had happened. They could scarcely believe their eyes, and it was not until Smith called to them by name and questioned them in regard to the happenings at Jamestown since his departure, that they were convinced he was himself. All were thin and gaunt, and they peered hungrily at the baskets of food the Indians bore. Most of them greeted Smith with genuine pleasure; others there were who frowned at the sight of him, who barely nodded a welcome, who answered him surlily and who got together in twos and threes to talk quickly as he passed on.

Smith led the way to the storehouse and bidding the Indians wait outside, he went within and persuaded the man in charge to permit him to take a number of articles. When he came out his arms were full of colored cloths and beads, steel knives and trinkets of many sorts. The Indians gave him their baskets to empty and he filled them with the presents, going back for iron pots and kettles of glistening brass. These he bade them carry to

Powhatan. To each of his guides he gave something for himself. Then speaking slowly, he said to Copotone:

"Kehaten Pokahontas patiaquagh niugh tanks manotyens neer mowmowchick rawrenock andowgh (bid Pocahontas bring hither two little baskets and I will give her white beads to make her a necklace)."

He would gladly have sent a message of thanks for her care of him that night, but he thought it best not to do so, since she might not wish it known that she had followed him.

"Pray her to come and see us soon," he added as he bade farewell to his guides whose eagerness to show their treasures at home was even greater than their curiosity to see further marvels.

After he had seen them safely outside of the palisades, Smith stopped to enquire by name for such men as had not come out to greet him.

"Oh! Ralph, he's dead and buried," they answered; and of another: "Christopher? He wore away from very weakness. And Robin went a sen'night ago with a quartain fever. This is no land for white men."

"But thou lookest hale and hearty. Captain," remarked one of the gentlemen, leaning against his door for support. "I'll wager the death thou didst face was not by starvation."

Then Smith learned in full the pitiful story of what the colony had suffered during his absence: lack of food and illness had carried off nearly half the colonists, and those that remained were weak and discouraged. Death had taken both of his enemies and of his friends, but some who had been opposed to him formerly had been brought to see during his absence how with his departure the life and courage of Jamestown had died down. Men there are—and most of them—who must ever be led by some one, and in Smith these adventurers had come to see a real leader of men.

While Smith stood questioning and heartening the downhearted, President Wingfield came out of his house on his way to the Government House. Smith doffed his hat and made a brave bow to honour, if not the man, at least the office he represented.

"So thou art returned. Captain Smith," said the President, coldly. "Methinks thou hast not fared so ill, better belike than most of us. Hast thou brought the provisions thou didst promise? We have been awaiting them somewhat anxiously. But first tell me where thou hast left Robinson and Emery, for the lives of our comrades, however humble, are of more value to us than even the sorely needed victuals."

Now Smith was aware that President Wingfield knew, as every other man in the colony knew, that Robinson and Emery were dead; the others had already discussed their fate with him. Therefore he realized that the President had some policy in putting such a question to him thus in public.

"Thou must have heard, sir, that they are dead," he replied. "Poor lads! Disobedience was the end of them. Had they but followed my commands they had returned alive to Jamestown many days ago; but they must needs land on the shore, instead of keeping in the stream as I bade them, and they were slain by the savages after I was captured."

"That is easily answered, Captain Smith," Wingfield solemnly remarked, and turning his head over his shoulder to speak as he walked off, he added: "The Council will require their lives at thy hands this day. See that thou art present in the Government House this afternoon at three by the clock to answer their questions."

"So that is what their next step is," Smith remarked to his friend Guy, a youth of much promise, as they walked off together. "They will accuse me of murder and try to hang me or to send me back to England in chains. But I have not been saved from death by a young princess to come to any such end, friend."

And as they walked to his house he told the story of his captivity and made plans for getting the better of those who sought to injure him.

The councillors, on their side, were not unanimous as to the course to adopt. Some were for putting him in safe-keeping—they did not mention the word imprisonment—until a ship should arrive and return with him to England. Others, who perhaps felt a doubt of their own ability to manage the settlement, were willing to acknowledge that they had misjudged him and suggested that at least he had better be given a chance to help them; and other timorous members, having witnessed the warmth of the greeting accorded him, advised that it would be wiser not to rush into any course of action which would displease the majority of the colonists. Thus it came to pass that Smith found the three o'clock meeting like a tiger that has had its claws drawn.

In the days that followed his spirit of encouragement, the willingness with which he put his shoulder to the wheel everywhere that aid was needed, his boldness in defying those leagued against him, completely changed the aspect of Jamestown. The gentlemen who had refused to wield axe or spade or bricklayer's trowel because of their gentility were shamed by his example.

"When Adam delved and Eve spanWho was then the gentleman?"

he demanded and swung the axe with lusty strokes against some hoary walnut tree.

But though he enjoyed the triumph over his enemies and the knowledge that his return, the provisions he had brought and the inspiration of his courage and activity were of great benefit to his fellows, nevertheless at times he experienced a feeling of loneliness. He thought of Pocahontas and wondered whether she would not come to Jamestown.

It was on a wintry day that Pocahontas made her first visit to the colony. Though they might lack most of the necessities of life, there was no scarcity of fuel. A huge bonfire was blazing at an open space where two streets were destined to meet in the future. Over some embers pulled away from the centre of the flame a pitch-kettle was heating and its owners, while waiting for its contents to melt, were warming a small piece of dried sturgeon. Around the bonfire sat John Smith and several gentlemen. He was pointing out to them on a rough chart the direction in which he thought the town should spread out when a new influx of colonists would need shelter. There were carpenters working on a house a few feet away, but their hammer blows did not ring out lustily as they should do when men are building with hope a new habitation; there was but little strength left in their arms.

When Smith looked up from his chart to indicate where a certain line should run, he saw standing before him the young Indian who had brought him Pocahontas's greeting after the night journey through the forest and who, he now realized, was the same fierce youth who had attempted his life at Werowocomoeo.

Claw-of-the-Eagle spoke:

"Werowance of the white men, Princess Pocahontas sends me to inform thee that she hath come to visit thee. E'en now she and her maidens await thee at the fort."

"She is most welcome," cried Smith, springing up. Then he called out in English: "Come, friends, and help me receive the daughter of Powhatan, who did save me at the risk of her own life. Give her a hearty English welcome."

"I WILL LEAD THE PRINCESS"

The colonists needed no urging. They were eager to see what an Indian princess looked like. But Smith outran them all and at the sight of the bright girlish face he stretched out his hands towards her as he would have done to an English maiden he knew well.

"Ah! little friend," he said coaxingly, "thou wilt not be angry with me longer. How much dost thou desire to make me owe thee, Pocahontas, my life, my freedom, my return home and now this pleasure?"

Pocahontas only smiled. Smith then turned, waving his hand to the men who had followed him.

"These, my comrades, would thank thee too could they but speak thy tongue."

The hats of cavaliers and the caps of the workmen were all doffed, and Pocahontas acknowledged their courtesy with great dignity.

"Let us show our guests our town," suggested Smith, "even though it lack as yet palaces and bazaars filled with gorgeous raiment. I will lead the princess; do ye care for her maidens and the young brave." As they walked along the path from the fort to Jamestown's one street he asked: "Tell me, my little jailor, how came The Powhatan to set me free? I have wondered every day since, and I cannot understand. Thou didst prevail with him, was it not so?"

"Aye," answered the girl. "First was I angry with thee, then my heart, though I did not wish to hearken to it, made me pity thee away from thy people, even as I pitied the wildcat I loosed from his trap. My father would not list to me at first, but I plead and reasoned with him, telling him that thy friendship for us would be even as a high tide that covereth sharp rocks over which we could ride safely."

"But what meant the songs and dances in the hut in the woods, Matoaka?"

"That was the ceremony of adoption. Thou art now the son of Powhatan and my brother. Thou wert taken into our tribe, and those were the ancient rites of our people."

"And the journey through the woods, didst thou fear for my safety then that thou didst follow all the way?"

But Pocahontas did not answer. She would not tell him that she had still doubted her father, and that she was not sure what instructions he had given the men ordered to guide the paleface.

"Thou art like the Sun God," said Smith with genuine feeling, "powerful to save and to bless, little sister—since I have been made thy brother. And as man may not repay the Sun God for all his blessings, no more may I repay thee for all thou hast done for me."

Pocahontas was on the point of replying when she suddenly burst out laughing at a sight before her. Two men who were rolling a barrel of flour from the storehouse to their own home let it slip from their weakened fingers. It rolled against one of the carpenters who was standing with his back to it, and hitting against his shins, sent him sprawling. It was undoubtedly a funny sight and she was not the only one to be amused. But the man did not rise.

"Why doth he not get up?" asked Pocahontas. "He cannot be badly hurt by such a light blow from that queer-shaped thing."

"I fear me he is too weakened by lack of food," answered Smith, gravely.

"Hath he naught to eat?" asked the girl in wide-eyed wonder. Then as if a strange thought had just come to her: "Is there not food for all? Must thou, too, my Brother, stint thyself?"

"In truth, little Sister, our rations are but short ones and if the ship cometh not soon from England with supplies, I fear me they must be shorter still."

"No!" she cried emphatically, shaking her head till her long braids swung to and fro, "ye shall not starve while there is plenty at Werowocomoco. This very night will I myself send provisions to thee. It hurts me here," and she laid her hand on her heart, "to think that thou shouldst suffer."

Just then President Wingfield and several officers of the Council, having heard the news of Pocahontas's visit, came toward them. They realized that the presence among them of this child, the best-loved daughter of the powerful Indian chieftain, was an important event. They did not quite know what to expect. Vague ideas of some Eastern queenly beauty, such as the Queen of Sheba or Semiramis, had led them to look for a certain royal magnificence of bearing and of garments, and they were taken aback to behold this slim young creature whose clothing in the eyes of some of them was inadequate. Nevertheless, they soon discovered that though she wore no royal purple nor jewels she bore herself with a dignity that was both maidenly and regal. They had hurriedly put on their own best collars and ruffs and to the eyes of the unsophisticated Indian girl they made a brave, though strange, appearance. She listened to their words of welcome and answered them through Smith's interpretation. But all the while she was taking in every detail of their costumes.

"We must give her presents," suggested one of the councillors as if discovering an idea that had come to no one else, and he sent a servant to fetch some of the trinkets which they had brought for the purpose of bartering with the savages.

Pocahontas forgot her dignity at the sight of them and clapped her hands in delight as Smith threw over her head a long chain of white and blue beads. Her pleasure was even greater when he held up a little mirror and she saw her face for the first time reflected in anything but a forest pool.

"Is that too for me?" she asked eagerly and clasped it to her breast when it was put into her hand, and then she peered into it from one side and the other, unwearied in making acquaintance with her own features.

The other maidens and Claw-of-the-Eagle were given presents also, but less showy ones. Smith went into his own little house and after hunting through his sea-chest, brought out a silver bracelet which he slipped on Pocahontas's arm, saying:

"This is to remind Matoaka always that she is my sister and that I am her brother."

It seemed to Pocahontas that she was incapable of receiving any further new impressions. It was as if her mind were a vessel filled to the brim with water that could not take another drop. Like a squirrel given more nuts than it can eat at once, who rushes to hide them away, her instinct made her long to take her treasures off where she could look at them alone.

"I go back to my father's lodge," she said and did not speak again till they reached the fort. Then when Smith had seen the little party beyond the palisades, she called back to him:

"Brother, I shall not forget. This night I will send thee food. I am well pleased with thy strange town and I will come again."

CHAPTER XII

POWHATAN'S AMBASSADOR

Pocahontas was as good as her word. That same evening as soon as she had exhibited her treasures to Powhatan and to his envious squaws and had related her impressions of the town and wigwams of the palefaces, she busied herself in getting together baskets of corn, haunches of dried venison and bear-meat and sent them by swift runners to "her brother" at Jamestown.

In the days following, though she played with her sisters, though she hunted with Nautauquas in the forest, though she listened at night, crouched against her father's knees before the fire to tales of achievements of her tribe in war, or to strange transformation of braves into beasts and spirits, her thoughts would wander off to the white man's island, to the many wonders it held which she had scarcely sampled. The pressure of her bracelet on her arm would recall its giver, and she saw again in her mind his eyes, so kind when they smiled on her, so stern at other times.

She thought too of the man she had seen rolled over by the barrel—of how slowly he had risen. She knew that there was such a thing as starvation, because sometimes allied tribes of the Powhatans, whose harvests had not been successful or whose braves had been lazy hunters, had come to beseech food from the great storehouse at Powhata. But she herself had never before seen any one faint for food, and it hurt her when she thought of the abundance at Werowocomoco, where not even the dogs went hungry, to know that there were men not far away who must go without. Her father made no objection when a day or two later she told him that she wished to take another supply of provisions to the white men.

"So be it," nodded Powhatan. "Thy captive shall be fed until the big canoe he said was on its way shall arrive. He saith—though this be great foolishness, since he cannot see so far—that at the end of this moon it will come safe over the waters. But until the day of its arrival, whenever that may be, thou canst send or carry of our surplus to them. And hearken, Matoaka," he whispered that the squaws might not hear, "thou hast wits beyond thy years, therefore do thou seek to learn some of the white man's magic. There be times when the cunning of the fox is worth more than the claws of the bear."

So every three or four days Pocahontas brought food to Smith, for his own need and for that of his fellows. Sometimes, accompanied by her sister or her maidens, she would go by night to Jamestown, and half laughing, half frightened, they would set down the baskets before the fort and run like timorous deer back to the forest before the sentinel had opened the gate in the palisade in answer to their call. Sometimes, with Claw-of-the-Eagle as her companion, she would walk through the street of Jamestown, greeting, now with girlish dignity, now with smiles, its inhabitants whose thin faces lighted up at sight of her. She came to symbolize to them the hope in the new world they had all but lost; they rejoiced to see her, not only for her gifts, but for herself.

They taught her to say after them a few words such as "Good-day," "food," and "the Captain," meaning Smith; and the possession of this new and strange accomplishment was almost as dear to her as beads or bracelet. The island for her was a place of enchantment. The sunset gun from the fort awoke more thrills of marvel in her than the rages of a thunderstorm; and the strangest medicine of all was the power the white men had of communicating their wishes to others at a distance by means of little marks upon scraps of paper.

One afternoon when she had come, accompanied by Cleopatra, she found the streets and houses of Jamestown deserted. As they wandered about, wondering what had happened to the palefaces, they heard the sound of voices issuing from a rough shed beyond. They seemed neither to be talking nor shrieking but chanting in a kind of rhythm such as she had never heard. Quietly the two maidens followed the sound to the shed. It was made of wood, open at the sides and roofed over with a piece of sail-cloth. Crouched behind some sumac bushes still bearing aloft their crimson torches, the girls looked on in wonderment, themselves unseen. The sun was sinking behind them, behind the backs too of the colonists who all faced the east. Then Pocahontas whispered to her sister:

"See, Cleopatra, they must be worshiping their Okee. Yon man all in white before them must be a shaman."

A keen curiosity kept her there, though Cleopatra pulled in fright at her skirt, whispering entreaties to be gone before some dire medicine should fall upon them. She saw them all, when the chanting had ceased, kneel down on the bare ground and heard them repeat some incantation which she felt sure must be of great strength, to judge by the firmness of the tone in which they all recited it. Their Okee, she thought, must be a very powerful one; and there came to her as she crouched there, the hidden witness of this evening service, the conviction that her father, if he would, and even with all his tribes, could never conquer this handful of determined men.

She was afraid that "her brother" might be angry with her for having looked on at ceremonies that were perhaps forbidden to women or members of other tribes; so, greatly to Cleopatra's relief, they slipped away, leaving at the fort the provisions they had borne on their strong young backs.

A few days later news came from Opechanchanough that the big canoe, so eagerly expected by the strangers, had been seen at Kecoughtan and was now on its way up the river. Powhatan was astounded, for it was the very day the white captain had foretold its arrival. Truly a man who could see so far across the waves of the big water was one to be feared. And from that day the werowance had deep respect for John Smith and his powers.

Now that the ship had brought provisions there was for a time no need of aid from Werowocomoco. But only for a time. One day when Smith had conducted Pocahontas over the ship to show her the wonders of this monster canoe, he asked her to have her people bring food once more to Jamestown.

VIRGINIA IN 1606—FROM CAPTAIN JOHN SMITH'S MAP

"The sailors of Captain Newport," he explained, "are staying here too long and are devouring much of the supplies designed for us. A strange mania hath overtaken them, little Sister; they are mad for gold. They believe that the streams about here are full of the dust they and our men of Jamestown value more than life itself. It is more to them than thy precious pocone, and as thou seest, they desert their ship and spend their days sifting sand. If they are not soon gone there will be nothing left for the mouths of any of us."

"Thou shalt not want, Brother," promised Pocahontas, and the next day came the Indians with large stores of provisions. These Smith now bought from them with beads and utensils and colored cloths. But the President and the Council, jealous of the growing importance of Smith's relations with the savages, sought to increase their own by paying four times the amount Smith had agreed upon.

Discouragement met Smith with each morning's sun and kept him awake at night. The colony seemed to take no root in this virgin soil; men who would not work in the fields to raise grain toiled feverishly in search of gold, forgetting that a full harvest would mean more for their welfare than bags of money. Then, to add to the troubles, a fire started one winter night at Jamestown and spread rapidly over most of the town, burning down the warehouse in which the precious grain was stored. From cold and starvation "more than halfe of us dyed," wrote Smith later in his history.

Both with his own strength and by his example John Smith strove to his utmost to rebuild Jamestown and to encourage the downhearted and to make friends for himself among those who had listened to suspicions of his purposes.

For a long time Powhatan had desired to secure weapons such as the white men used, but the colonists had so far refused the Indians' request to barter them. Now he determined to try other methods. He sent twenty fat turkeys—each a heavy burden for the man who bore it across his shoulders—to Captain Newport, asking that in return the Englishman would send him twenty swords. Newport, whose orders from the authorities in London had been not to offend the natives in any manner, had not refused and had sent the swords in return. Then Powhatan, still eager to secure a further store of weapons, had twenty more fine turkeys carried to Smith, asking for twenty swords more. But Smith, who had been taught by experience and insight many things about the relations which should prevail between the colony and the Indians, knew how unwise it was to give to an untried friend the means of turning against the giver. He knew that the Indians respected his sternness with them more than they did the evident desire of Newport and the Council to please them. Therefore he refused. The disappointed savages showed their anger and cried out insolent words against Smith.

Finding they could not weaken his decision, they sought to steal the swords. They were discovered and Smith, realizing that the time had come when a decided stand must be taken, had them whipped and imprisoned.

Some of the Council protested, declaring that this was the wrong way to treat the Indians and urged that Powhatan was sure to resent their action. How did Smith know, they asked, that these savages were acting at the command of their chief? Was it not merely a sudden impulse of anger that had led them to take what ought to have been given them?

But the prisoners, who believed in Smith's power to read the past as well as the future, thinking it useless to try to hide the truth from him, confessed that Powhatan had commanded them to secure the swords by any method. Powhatan was now aware that his plan had failed and that it was necessary for him to disavow the deed of his messengers. To convince the palefaces of his good faith he must send some one to talk with them whom they would trust. And so it was that Pocahontas went to Jamestown as ambassadress.

Accompanied by slaves bearing presents of food, seed corn for the spring planting and pelts of deer and bear and wildcat, Pocahontas was received at Jamestown with much ceremonial.

"I bear these gifts from The Powhatan," she said to Smith, who always acted as interpreter. "He begs thee to excuse him of the injuries done by some rash ontoward captains his subjects, desiring their liberties for this time with the assurance of his love forever."

The manner in which she delivered this little speech was so frank that Smith knew she was ignorant of her father's real part in the theft. The men had had their lesson, and Powhatan his warning, therefore clemency might be effectively dispensed.

"Dost thou desire, Matoaka, that these men should be freed?"

"Oh, yes, my Brother," she replied eagerly. "Thou knowest thyself how the trapped man or beast pines to escape. My heart is sad at the thought of any creature kept in durance."

"And yet, little Sister," answered Smith gravely, while he watched her quick change of expression, "I needs must deliver up these prisoners of mine to another gaoler, to one who will treat them as sternly as thou didst treat me at Werowocomoco."

Pocahontas's drawn brows indicated her endeavor to understand his meaning.

"Wilt *thou* be their gaoler, Matoaka?" he asked; and she, suddenly comprehending his joke, laughed aloud.

The men were given into her custody and on her return home Powhatan was much pleased with his daughter's embassy.

In September of that year Smith at last was made in name, what he had long been in fact, the head of the colony. As President he could now carry out his plans with less opposition. The building of new houses and the church went on briskly; the training of men in military exercises, the exploration of the shores of Chesapeake Bay—all these received his attention. Master Hunt, the clergyman, whose library had been burned in the fire, spent his time in encouraging the colonists, and twice each day he held his services in the church for whose altar he melted candles and gathered wild flowers.

In London the governors of the Colony had decided it would be a wise thing to attach Powhatan still closer to the English settlement. Their ideas of the position and character of an Indian potentate were very vague indeed. They had been told that all savages were fond as children are of bright colored dress and ornaments. So they reasoned that of course this Indian chieftain of thirty tribes would be delighted with the regal pomp of a coronation. They sent orders by the *Phoenix*—a ship laden with stores which arrived that summer—that Powhatan should be brought to Jamestown and crowned there with the crown they shipped over for that purpose.

Smith, knowing Powhatan as none of the other colonists did, was not in favor of this plan. It did not seem to him that a crown instead of a feather headdress would make any difference to the werowance, whose power among his own people needed no external decoration to strengthen it. But he had no choice but to obey, so he and Captain Waldo and three other gentlemen, went to Werowocomoco to bring Powhatan back with them.

On their arrival they found the werowance absent, whether by chance or by policy. By this time Powhatan had lost some of his first awe of the white men's wits and had concluded it was worth while to try and meet strangers' wiles with wiles of his own.

"Where thinkest thou he can have gone?" asked Waldo. "I like it not. Smith; mayhap he is e'en now preparing some mischief against us."

"I wish we had not harkened to thee. Captain Smith," said one of the gentlemen, glancing nervously over his shoulder; "it was a fool's wisdom to come thus without good yeomen with match-locks to frighten away their arrows."

"Gentlemen," replied Smith, showing his vexation in his tone, "I tell ye ye are in no danger if ye do not yourselves bring it about with your looks of suspicion. Remember that all Werowocomoco is feasting its eyes upon us, and bear yourselves as Englishmen should."

"Where was it they nearly brained thee, Captain?" queried the fourth. "And not even thy friend, the little princess, is here to welcome thee. Doth not her absence cause thee some anxiety?"

It did in truth set John Smith to wondering. He did not fear that any harm was planned, but Pocahontas's absence was unexpected and he wondered what its significance might be. He had been looking forward to seeing his little sister again in her own home and had expected to enjoy a talk with her which would not be interrupted as their conversations in Jamestown always were by the many demands upon his time and attention. Now that he was so much more familiar with her language, it was a pleasure to discover what a maiden of the forests thought of her own world and that strange world he had brought to touch hers.

The Indians who had come forward to welcome the white men now pointed to a small meadow at the edge of the trees. They did not reply to Smith's questions as to what he was to do there, but knowing that this spot was sometimes used for special purposes. Smith led the way.

"Whither are we bound. Captain?" asked Andrew Buckler querulously. "It doth not seem wise to go further off from our boat. If they mean harm to us we shall have all the longer way to fight through."

"There will be no fighting to be done," declared Smith, not deigning even to slacken his gait.

But just then loud shrieks came from the woods, and between the trees dashed out a score or more creatures directly upon them.

CHAPTER XIII

POWHATAN'S CORONATION

The trees grew so close together that it was difficult for the Englishmen to distinguish in the shadows they cast the figures whirling between the trunks. Half naked they were: here a mass of something painted red; there flashed a white arm, of a whiteness such as nature never dyed, and there issued shoulders of a brilliant blue, as they advanced dancing and shrieking.

"All their war paint on!" ejaculated Captain Waldo.

And in that moment John Smith lost his faith in the friendship Powhatan had sworn to him, and he drew his sword, ready to pierce the first oncomer.

Then he looked again ... and hastily thrust his sword back into its scabbard, shouting to his comrades who had also drawn their blades, "Hold!"

For there before him, the first of the dancers who had run out of the forest, advanced Pocahontas! On her head she wore branching antlers, an otter skin at her waist and one across her arm, a quiver at her back, and she carried a bow and arrow in her hand. In a flash she realized what the Englishmen were thinking—that they were caught in an ambush.

"My Brother!" she cried out in a tone that rang with disappointment, "didst thou too doubt me? Tell them, thy companions, that I lay my life in their hands if any harm was intended."

Seldom in his life had John Smith felt so at a loss as to what he should reply. He hurriedly explained to the others that Pocahontas was evidently intending to do them special honour in welcoming them with some kind of sylvan masque. Then facing her, he cried:

"Forgive us, Matoaka, and be not angry that we mistook thy kindness. See, we seat ourselves here upon the ground and we beseech thee that thou and thy maidens will continue thy songs and thy dancing, which will greatly divert us."

Pocahontas's disappointment vanished at once and she sped back with her comrades to the woods, where they repeated their masque, this time to the amusement of the Englishmen, who were somewhat ashamed to think that they had been so frightened by a troop of girls. All of the dancers were horned like their leader and the upper parts of their bodies and their arms were painted red, white or blue. There was a fire blazing in the centre of the field and around this they formed a ring, dancing and singing a song which, while unlike anything Smith's companions had ever heard, affected their pulses like drumbeats. Some of the words they sang Smith was able to catch words of welcome, songs of young maidens in which they told of the joys of childhood and of the days when sweet-hearts would seek them and when they would follow some brave to his wigwam.

Pocahontas, he thought, was as graceful as a young roe; her feet were as quick as the flames of the fire, and every now and then, from the very exuberance of her happiness, she shot an arrow over their heads into the trees beyond. Smith could not help wondering what kind of a husband she would follow home some day.

The masque lasted an hour; all the different motions were symbolic, as Smith had learned all Indian dances were, and much of it he was able to comprehend. In any case he would have enjoyed the masque, knowing that Pocahontas had performed it to honour her father's guests. When it was over, suddenly as they had come, the maidens vanished into the dark forest.

The Englishmen were not left alone, however, for during the dancing a number of braves and squaws had come to look on at the ceremony and even more at the audience. Now Nautauquas came forward and greeted Smith.

"My father hath just returned. He hurried back when he learned that ye were to visit him. He hath had the guest lodge prepared and awaits your coming there."

Powhatan greeted them when they entered the lodge, which Smith recognized at once as the one where his life had been in such jeopardy.

"Tell them they are welcome, thy comrades," he said to Smith, "and thou, my son, art always as one of mine own people."

They seated themselves on the mats spread for them, and the usual feasting began, the Englishmen doing more than justice to the Indian dishes.

"'Tis a strange beast and of a rare flavor withal, this raccoon," said Waldo, "and methinks the King at Westminster hath no better trencher meat. Hath the old savage asked of thee yet our errand, Smith?"

"An Indian never asks the errand of his guest," he replied; "but now we have eaten it is not meet that I delay longer to tell him."

He rose to his feet and began to speak. Pocahontas, who had stood at the entrance looking in, now entered and sat down at her father's feet.

"Ruler of many tribes, Werowance of the Powhatans, Wahunsunakuk, we have come to bring the greetings sent thee from across the sea by our own great werowance, James. With the English, the Spaniards, the French and other great peoples beyond the seas, their greatest chief who rules many tribes is called a 'king.' He is mightier than all other werowances, hath always much riches and honour, and when the time comes that, by the death of an old king or by conquest, a new king takes his place, he is crowned. They put a circlet upon his head and in his hand they place a staff of honour and upon his shoulders they throw royal robes, so that all who see shall know that this is the King and that all must do him fealty. Our own King James, who hath heard of thee, and of the many tribes that are subject to thee, hath desired that thou, too, shouldst be crowned as another king, his friend, so that the English may know that he calls thee 'brother,' and that thine own people shall hold thee in yet greater awe."

Powhatan manifested no sign of interest in these words; but from the eager look on Pocahontas's face Smith was aware that his Indian speech had at least been comprehended.

"Therefore," Smith continued, "it is planned to hold thy coronation at Jamestown upon as near a day as thou shalt see fit to appoint. Our King hath sent presents for thee which await thy coming to us."

Then he ceased and looked to Powhatan for an answer. The werowance thought a moment in silence, then he spoke:

"If your king hath sent me presents, I also am a king, and this is my land; eight days I will stay to receive them. Your Father is to come to me, not I to him, nor yet to your fort."

He spoke with so kingly a dignity that the Englishmen did not seek to dissuade him. They promised to do as he wished and to persuade Newport, whom he called their "father," to go to Werowocomoco, which might be considered as Powhatan's capital. Then they departed for Jamestown, after having thanked Powhatan and Pocahontas for their entertainment.

Pocahontas awaited their return with eagerness. She talked the matter over with Nautauquas. Perhaps, she said, there was some strange medicine in this ceremony which would make their father invulnerable and perchance safe even from death itself.

"I have more faith in the white men's guns than in their medicine," declared Claw-of-the-Eagle. "Ever since one of those fat housebuilders whom they call Dutchmen let me try to fire off one of them, I know now that they are not worked by magic. If we could manage to get enough of them we should be ten times as strong as their starving company and could destroy all of them before another shipload of newcomers arrived."

"Nay," cried Pocahontas, "not as long as our brother, the captain, lives. Thou couldst not even face his eyes when he is angry."

She did not imagine that she was stating an actual fact. Claw-of-the-Eagle had never been able to look Smith in the eye since he crawled away from the lodge where he had meant to kill the white man. It was only Smith himself who awed him so; but he dreamed that some day he might be able to deal a blow in the dark when those terrible eyes could not stop him. In the meantime he felt equal to meeting the other palefaces day or night.

"But," asked Nautauquas slowly and gravely, as if weighing the matter, "why should we wish to destroy these white men? I once had different thoughts, and I have gone alone into the forest and fasted and prayed to Okee that I might know whether to greet them as foe or friend. In some way the white tribes that live across the great waters have found their way westward. Many have come, the rumor is, to the south of us, men of different race and different tongue from these on the island. These others are cruel to the Indians among whom they have settled and have destroyed many villages and made captive their braves and squaws. Now I have talked with our father, Wahunsunakuk, of what I now speak, since we can no longer hope to hide our trail again to these wanderers from the rising sun, that it is better to make friends of these who have come and who seem well-disposed towards us, and to have them for allies rather than enemies."

In spite of himself, Claw-of-the-Eagle was impressed with this reasoning.

"Dost thou then like these paleface strangers and their ways?" he asked.

"There is much about them I do not understand," replied Nautauquas; "how they can wear so many garments; why they build them houses that let in no air; why they come here when they have villages beyond the seas; yet I know that they are brave and that their medicine is mighty."

Pocahontas spoke little. She had never told anyone how much interest she found in all that concerned the white men and their ways.

It was some days later that Smith, Captain Newport and fifty men started to march to Werowocomoco for the coronation of Powhatan. The presents which the King and the governors of the Colony in London had chosen for him were sent by boat up the river. When the company of Englishmen in their farthingale-breeches, slashed sleeves and white ruffs, their swords and buckles glistening, accompanied by a few soldiers bearing halberds and long muskets, arrived, the entire population of the village and those of other villages for leagues about were awaiting them. Braves and squaws had decked themselves out also in their choicest finery—necklaces and beads and embroidered robes.

It was a wonderful picture that the dark surrounding forest looked upon— the group of gaily colored Indians facing the more soberly dressed Europeans. Round them circled children, pushing, peering between their elders that they might miss nothing. And through it all, running from one group to the other, welcoming, explaining, smiling and laughing, flitted the white-clad Pocahontas.

After their greeting, when Powhatan and Captain Newport eyed each other appraisingly, the gifts were brought into the field where Pocahontas had danced her masque and spread out before the curious gaze of the savages. Pocahontas, in her white doeskin skirt and wearing many strings of white and blue beads, went about among her new friends, and laid her hand into that of Captain Newport, as Smith had told her was the manner in which the English greeted one another. Some of the chieftains scowled at the sight and did not relish the friendliness shown by her to the strangers. Several even remonstrated with Powhatan who, however, would not restrain her. After a few words with Smith, she rejoined Cleopatra and others of her sisters at one side of the field.

"What is yon curious thing, Pocahontas?" they questioned of her superior knowledge, as the wrappings were taken off a bedstead that Captain Newport by means of signs presented solemnly to Powhatan.

"That," she answered, having had a glimpse of such furniture at Jamestown, "that is a couch on which they sleep."

"Is it more comfortable than our mats?" asked Cleopatra. "I should fear to fall out of it into the fire."

Plainly Powhatan, too, was at a loss to know what to do with it. The next gifts, a basin and ewer, met with more enthusiasm. The squaws were particularly interested in them when Pocahontas told them that they were made of a substance which would not break as did their own vessels of sun-baked pottery. But it was the red mantle of soft English cloth, in shape like to the one, he was told. King James had worn at his coronation at Westminster, that made Powhatan's grim features relax a little with pleasure. Captain Newport placed it on the werowance's shoulders and held a mirror that he might behold himself thus handsomely apparelled.

Then they proceeded to the crowning. Newport would have liked to have some words of ritual read, even though the principal of the ceremony had not been able to understand them; but the chaplain pointed out that neither the law nor the Prayer-Book made any provision for the crowning of a heathen, and that after all it was the act, not the words, which would impress the savages.

The drummer beat a loud tattoo and the trumpeter blew a call that startled the squaws and the children into shrieks; the braves were quicker in hiding their astonishment. Then Smith and Newport walked forward, Newport holding the crown. Smith said:

"Kneel, Wahunsunakuk, that we may crown thee."

But Powhatan, whose understanding of these strange proceedings was not clear, though he comprehended Smith's words, continued to stand stiff and straight as a pine tree.

"Kneel down, oh, Powhatan," urged Smith. "Mistake not, this act is a kingly one; so do all the kings of Europe."

But Powhatan would not. To him the posture was one unfitting to the dignity of a mighty werowance, ruler over thirty tribes and lord of sixty villages. He would accept presents sent him, and he had no objection to wearing a glittering ring upon his head if the white men chose to give him one; but he would not kneel; that was going too far in his acquiescence to strange ways. Such a position was for suppliants and squaws and children.

Smith was uncertain what to do. The officers of the Colony in London had laid great stress upon a proper crowning, believing, as he did not, that it would impress the Indians as the symbol of an alliance between their people and the English. He thought a moment, then whispered a word to Newport. The two quickly laid their hands on Powhatan's shoulders and pressed down gently but firmly, a pressure which bowed his knees slightly. Then, before he had time to recover himself, Newport had placed the crown upon his grizzled head.

According to orders, two soldiers, seeing that the ceremony was accomplished, fired a salute with their muskets. Powhatan started suddenly; Nautauquas raised his head like a deer scenting danger, and some of the braves started to run towards the knot of white men. But the calm demeanor of Smith showed them their error.

"We are quits," said Captain Waldo to Buckler; "the maids frightened us with their masks and we have frightened their braves with our muskets."

Powhatan in the red robe and crown seated himself upon the mats that were brought out to him, and Smith whispered to one of the gentlemen who had accompanied him:

"In faith, Radcliffe, is he not more kingly looking than our royal James?"

The idea of a coronation had seemed absurd to him, and he had believed that the old chief would appear ridiculous decked out in mock finery, but he admitted to himself that such was far from being the case.

Then the feast was brought on and the Englishmen again did full justice to the Indian dishes. Pocahontas came and sat beside Smith.

"Welcome, little Sister," he said, "and how dost thou like thy father's new robes?"

"He appeareth strange to me," she answered, "but he will not wear them long. It is beautiful, that cloak, but he can paint his flesh as fine a color with pocone, and it will not be so warm nor so heavy."

Smith laughed.

"Wouldst thou not like to try to wear clothes such as our women wear? Perchance thou mayst try what they are like before long, for soon we shall be seeing white squaws come over on the ships."

"Do white men have squaws, too?" asked Pocahontas in astonishment.

"For a surety. Didst thou think Englishmen could live forever without wife or chick at their hearths?"

"And thou, my Brother," she queried eagerly, "will thy squaw and thy children come soon?"

"I have none, Matoaka; my trails have led through so many dangers that I have not taken a squaw."

"But a squaw would not fear danger if thou couldst take her with thee, or if not, she would wait in thy lodge ready to welcome thee on thy return. She would have soft skins ready for thy leggings, new mats for thee to sleep upon; she would point out all the stores of dried venison she had hung on her tent-pole while thou wert gone, and fresh sturgeon would she cook for thee and prepare walnut-milk for thy thirst."

"'Tis a pretty picture thou drawest, Matoaka," he answered, yet he did not laugh at it. "Often I feel lonely in my wigwam and I wonder if some day I shall not bring a wife into it."

"There would be none who would refuse thee," answered the girl simply.

Smith did not take in the significance of her words, yet his thoughts were of her. Suppose he should throw in his lot altogether with this new country and take for wife this happy, free child of the aboriginal forest? It was only a passing thought. He had not time to consider it further, for Newport had risen and gave the signal for them to start on the return march to Jamestown. He rose, too, and bade farewell to Pocahontas.

During the feasting Powhatan had been thinking over what he meant to do. Gravely he presented to Captain Newport a bundle of wheat ears for spring planting; then with the utmost dignity, he handed him the moccasins and the fur mantle he had laid aside when they placed his coronation robe upon him. Newport received them in amazement, not knowing what he was to do with them; but Smith made a speech of thanks for him.

"What did the old savage mean?" asked Newport as they were on their homeward way. "Was it because he wanted to give a present in return?"

"Methinks," answered Smith, "that Powhatan hath a sense of humor and doth wish to show us that his coronation hath so increased his importance that his cast-off garments have perforce won new value in our eyes."

CHAPTER XIV

A DANGEROUS SUPPER

Some months later, the first of the year 1609, there was again grave danger of starvation at Jamestown, and Smith, remembering the full storehouses at Werowocomoco, determined to go and purchase from Powhatan what was needed. Taking with him twelve men, they set out by boat up the river.

"I doubt not," said John Russell as they sailed along the James, now no longer muddy as in the summer but coated with bluish ice in the shallows, "I doubt not that those fat Dutchmen the Council sent over to build a house for Powhatan—what need hath he of a Christian house?—have grown fatter than ever upon his good victuals while we be wasting thinner day by day."

"I have no liking for those foreigners," exclaimed Ratcliffe, watching with greedy eyes a flock of redhead ducks that flew up from one of the little bays as the boat approached, wishing he could shoot them for his dinner. "Were there not enough carpenters and builders in Cheapside and Hampstead that the lords of the Colony must needs hunt out these ja-speaking lubbers from Zuider-Zee? They have no love for us, no more than we for them. If they thought 'twould vantage them, they would not scruple to betray us to the savages."

As they proceeded up the James, away from tidewater, the ice extended farther out into the river, until when they neared Werowocomoco there was a sheet of it that stretched half a mile out from shore. Smith had determined, so desperate was the plight of the colonists, that he would not go back to Jamestown without a good supply of corn and other food. He hoped that Powhatan would consent to his buying it; but he meant to take it by force if necessary. For some time there had been little intercourse between the English and the Indians; the latter had seemed more unwilling to barter stores, and there was a rumor that Powhatan had new grievances against the white men.

The four Dutchmen who for some weeks had been building the house for Powhatan, had discussed amongst themselves the relative advantages of friendship with the werowance or with the English. They decided that to weaken the latter would be their best policy, since they would be content to see the struggling settlement of Europeans destroyed and to entrust their own fate to the savages. There was much in the Indian method of living which pleased them; plenty of good food and full pipes of tobacco and squaws to serve them. So they laid their plans and imparted to Powhatan in confidence that Smith, who they knew must soon appear in search of supplies, was in reality using this need as a pretext and that he meant to fire upon the Indians and do great damage to Werowocomoco.

Pocahontas did not overhear this talk, but she had watched the four strangers together and her sharp ears had frequently caught the word "Smith" repeated. Now when the news was shouted through the lodges that the boat bearing Smith and his companions was approaching slowly through the broken ice, Pocahontas hurried eagerly to the river and waved her hand to her friends. She watched them come ashore but checked herself as she started to run to meet them. She had a feeling that this was not the moment for pretty speeches, and feared that Powhatan's enmity to the English had been fanned by the Dutchmen until it was ready to burst forth. She determined, instead of showing any interest in the strangers, to appear indifferent to them and to let her people think she had grown hostile to them. She would stay close to her father in order to learn what he intended to do.

The werowance as he came towards them did not wear his red mantle nor his crown of English make, but a headdress of eagle feathers and leggings and a cape of brown bear fur. Perhaps he wished to show that he had no need to wear a crown to look a king. He strode slowly to the river and called out in greeting to the white men:

"Ye are welcome to Werowocomoco, my son, but why comest thou thus with guns when thou visiteth thy father?"

"We be come to buy food from thee, oh Powhatan," answered Smith, "to fill thy hands and those of thy people with precious beads and knives and cloths of many colors for thy squaws in exchange for food for to-day and to last till comes nepinough (the earing of the corn), when we shall harvest the fruit of the seed we plant."

"But lay aside first your arms. What need have ye of arms who come upon such a peaceful purpose? Have ye thought to try to frighten my people to sell thee of their stores? What will it avail you to take by force what you may quickly have by love, or destroy them that provide you food? Every year our friendly trade will furnish you with corn, and now also, if you will come in friendly manner to see us, and not thus with your guns and swords as to invade your foes."

Many of the English, when Smith had translated word after word of the chief's discourse, felt shamed at the show of force their weapons manifested, and would have been willing to lay them by while they were upon the land of this friendly chieftain, whom, they felt, they had misjudged. But Smith was not deceived. He was learning to read the signs of Indian ways, and he knew that the chief had reasons for desiring to see them unarmed. So he called out in answer:

"Your people coming to Jamestown are entertained with their bows and arrows without any exceptions, we esteeming it proper with you as it is with us, to wear our arms as part of our apparel."

There followed more words between the two and much talk of "father" and "son"; but Pocahontas, who listened to it all, was not easy. She had given her affection to Smith since the day she saved his life, and now she was sure that her father planned to harm him. Nautauquas was away with Claw-of-the-Eagle on a foray against the Massawomekes, the latter having sworn to her that he would now accomplish deeds to make the chiefs of his tribe declare him worthy to be called a real Powhatan brave. Had her brother been at Werowocomoco, she might have confided her fear to him; as it was, she realized that she alone must discover her father's intentions.

She saw that Powhatan had withdrawn on some pretext she did not overhear and that Smith, standing at the entrance of the lodge which Powhatan had assigned to the English, was chatting with some of the squaws he remembered from the time of his captivity, while the rest of the white men were busy in carrying the objects they had brought for bartering from the boat to the lodge.

Suddenly a number of Indian braves rushed towards him, arrows notched in the bowstrings. The foremost savage let his arrow fly; it was aimed a few feet too high and, grazing Smith's steel morion, hit the bark of the lodge-covering above his head. The squaws, shrieking loudly, took to their heels. Smith, before another arrow left its bow, whipped out his pistol and pointed it at the advancing crowd. Then John Russell, hearing the commotion, rushed from the lodge. Pressing the snaphance of his musket, he fired into the oncoming savages, but failed to hit one.

Nevertheless, the Indians, seeing that the Englishmen were still armed, turned and fled, disappearing into the forest. Pocahontas, trembling with anger, ran through the trees to find her father to ask him what was the meaning of this treacherous treatment of his guests.

After she had run some little distance she caught sight of Powhatan approaching and, hiding behind a rock, she waited to see whither he was bound. To her amazement, she saw that he was turning to the strangers' lodge and that behind him followed slaves bearing great baskets of food and seed-corn. What could he mean, she wondered, by first trying to kill and then to feast the white men? She followed, herself unseen, while Powhatan approached Smith without the slightest hesitation.

"It rejoiceth my heart, my son," she heard him call out when he was within one hundred feet of where Smith was standing, watching him with puzzled eyes, "to know that thou art unharmed. While I was gone to see that provisions were provided for thee, even according to my word, my young men who were crazed with religious zeal and fasting they have undergone in preparation for a great ceremonial planned by our priests, knew not what they were doing. See, my son, think no evil of us; would we at one moment seek to harm and to help thee? Behold the supplies I, thy father, have here for thee."

And Smith, though he doubted somewhat, did not feel certain that Powhatan was not speaking the truth. But Pocahontas, still in hiding, knew well that no man in Werowocomoco would have dared shoot at the white men except by direct order of their werowance.

Perhaps, however, all was now well; perhaps her father had at least realized that the Englishmen were not to be caught napping. She looked on while Powhatan and Smith superintended the placing of the great piles of stores in the boat and the refilling of the baskets with the goods with which the Englishmen paid for them.

Then, their work over, the Indians began to deck themselves out in the beads and cloths. While they were thus occupied a man came running and dropped down exhausted before Powhatan, able to gasp out a couple of words only. Though the messenger had not breath enough to cry them out, they were heard by the Indians standing nearby and shouted aloud. Immediately the crowd jumped to their feet and uttering loud shrieks, danced up and down and around in circles, to the sound of rattles and drums.

"What is the meaning of all this, Smith?" asked Russell, who with the other white men stood watching the strange performance.

"Tell them, my son," said Powhatan, understanding from the tone of the Englishman's voice that his words were a question, "that two score of my braves, among them Nautauquas and Claw-of-the-Eagle, have won a great victory over one hundred of our enemies, and that this is our song of triumph."

The old chief's eye shone more brightly than ever, and his back was as firm and straight as that of one of his sons.

"I shall soon have witnessed all their different dances," John Smith confided to Russell, when he had repeated Powhatan's explanation. "There lacks now only the war dance."

There was a pause in the dance; then Powhatan gave a signal. Drums and rattles started up once more. The rhythm was a different one, even the white men could tell this; and they noticed that the savages moved more swiftly as if animated by the greatest excitement. Fresh dancers, their faces and bodies painted in red and black, took the places of those who fell from fatigue, and the woods resounded with their loud song.

"It must have been a great victory," suggested Ratcliffe, "to have excited them in this manner."

But Pocahontas's heart beat as if it were the war drum itself, for she knew what the white men did not know, that this last was a war dance; but she was not yet certain against whom her tribe was to take the war-path. She must wait and see.

At last the dancing ceased and the feasting began, and the Englishmen still watched with interest the "queer antics" of the savages, as they called them. All was now so peaceful that they laid aside their weapons, setting a guard to watch them, and sitting about the great fire they had built in the lodge, waited for the morning's high tide to lift their boat out of the half-frozen ooze in which the ebb had left it. Powhatan and the Indians had withdrawn, but the werowance had sent a messenger with a necklace and bracelet of freshwater pearls with words of affection for "his son" and to say that he would shortly send them supper from his own pots, that they might want for nothing that night.

The darkness had come quickly and the woods that stretched between the lodge and the centre of Werowocomoco were thick and sombre. Through them Pocahontas sped more swiftly than she had ever run a race with her brothers. She did not trip over the roots slippery with frost nor, though she had not taken time to put a mantle over her bare shoulders, did she feel the cold. For she knew now that the war dance had been danced against the English.

She was all but breathless when she reached the lodge near the river's edge, but rushing inside, she seized a musket from the pile on the ground, to the astonishment of the guard, who recognized her in time not to hurt her, and thrust it into Smith's hands, crying:

"Arm yourselves, my friends. Make ready quickly," and as Smith would have questioned, she panted: "When your weapons are in readiness then will I speak."

Smith gave hurried orders, reproaching himself for his false confidence. The men sprang up from the fire, seized their long-barrelled muskets and their halberts; and a few who had laid aside their steel corselets hastily fastened them on again, and threw their bandoliers, filled with charges, over their shoulders. The merry, careless party was now quickly converted into a troop of cautious soldiers. Then Smith turned to Pocahontas, whose breath was coming more quietly as she beheld the precautions taken for defence. She answered his unspoken query:

"I overheard the words of the treacherous Dutchmen to my father even now. I feared when I heard the war song and saw them dancing the war dance. Woe is me! my Brother, that I should speak against my own father, but I listened to the plans he hath made to take you here unawares, your weapons out of your hands. For this moment he hath waited all day and he hath sought to deceive you with fair words. They are now on their way with the supper he promised thee; then when you are all eating he hath given orders to his men that they fall upon you and slay all, that none may escape. And so as soon as I learned this, that thou to whom he had sworn friendship and thine were in dire peril, I hastened through the dark forest to warn thee."

Smith was deeply touched by this manifestation of her loyalty. He knew the danger she ran if Powhatan should learn of what she had done.

"Matoaka," he cried, clasping her hand, "thou hast this night put all England in thy debt. As long as this Virginia is a name men remember, so long will men recall how thou didst save her from destruction. In truth, thy father had lulled my suspicions to sleep, and hadst thou not come to warn us we had surely perished. The thanks of all of us to thee. Princess," he continued, when he had turned and told his astonished men the gist of her words, "and to my little Sister my own deep gratitude again."

He loosened a thick gold chain from about his neck, one that he had brought back from the country of the Turks, and put it about her bare neck.

"Take this chain in remembrance," he said. Then his comrades pressed forward, each with some gift they emptied into the maiden's hands.

She gazed at them all lovingly, but she shook her head slowly, the tears falling as she said:

"I dare not, my friends; if my father should behold these gifts he would kill me, since he would know that it was I who had brought ye warning."

Slowly she took off the chain and reluctantly placed in it Smith's hand, and let gently fall the other treasures she longed to keep. Smith bent and kissed her hand as reverently as he had once kissed that of Good Queen Bess.

Pocahontas started. "I hear them coming," she cried, and with one bound she had sprung forth again into the night, skirting the river until she was sure of reaching her lodge without running into the troop of Indians advancing with dishes and baskets of food, who, however, were not slaves but braves and armed.

When these reached the stranger-lodge they brought in the supper and laid it down with apparent great heartiness that is the few who actually bore the baskets. The others found themselves somehow halted by Smith at the entrance and engaged in ceremonious conversation. When they suggested that the white men lay aside their weapons and seat themselves the better to enjoy their food, Smith replied that it was the custom of the English at night always to eat standing, food in one hand and musket in the other. For a long time this parleying went on; Smith would not show that he had discovered their perfidy.

Then the baffled Indians retired to the forest, to await the moment when they could catch the white men off guard. But though all night they spied about the lodge, not once did they find the sentinels away from their posts, and they had too much fear of the "death tubes" to attempt an onslaught on men so well defended.

So, thanks to Pocahontas, the morning dawned on an undiminished number of English, and at high tide they embarked in their boat and returned to Jamestown with their provisions so precariously won.

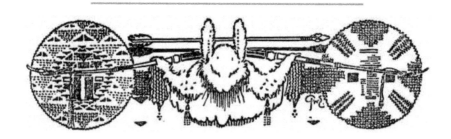

CHAPTER XV

A FAREWELL

The late summer sun was beating down pitilessly upon the lodges and open spaces of Werowocomoco. Even the children were quiet in the shade, covering their heads with the long green blades of the maize, plaiting the tassels idly and humming the chant of the Green Corn Festival they had celebrated some weeks before. The old braves smoked or dozed in their wigwams, and the squaws left their pounding of corn and their cooking until a cooler hour. The young braves only, too proud to appear affected by any condition of the weather, made parade of their industry and sat fashioning arrow-heads or ran races in the full sunshine, till a wise old chief called out to them that they were young fools with no more sense than blue jays.

Off in the woods, near a hollow in a little stream where the trout and crawfish disported themselves over a bright sandy bottom, Pocahontas lay at full length, her brown arms stretched out, the color of the pine needles beneath them. The leafage of a gigantic red oak shaded her; through its greenery she could see the heavy white clouds, and once an eagle flying as it seemed straight up into the sun. Away from its direct rays, cooled by her bath in the stream and clad in an Indian maiden's light garb, she was rejoicing in the summer heat. She enjoyed the sleepy feeling that dulled the woodland sights and sounds: the tapping of a woodpecker on a distant tree, the occasional call of a catbird, the soft scurrying of a rabbit or a squirrel, the buzzing of a laden bee—all mingled into one melody of summer of which she did not consciously distinguish the individual notes. Just as pleasantly confused were her thoughts, pictures of which her drowsiness blurred the outlines, so that she passed with no effort from the flecked stream she had just left to the moonlit field she and her maidens had encircled a few nights before, chanting harvest songs. She saw, too, the supple bend of Claw-of-the-Eagle's body as he had waited for the signal to bound forward in the race at Powhata when he outran the others; and then she seemed again to see him run the day Wansutis saved him from being clubbed to death.

As if the many deeds of violence done that day called up others of their kind, she saw, and did not shrink from seeing, the fate of the Dutchmen at Werowocomoco who had sought to betray Smith to Powhatan. Her father, angered at them, had had them brained upon the threshold of the house they had built for him.

Then the thoughts of Pocahontas found themselves at Jamestown, whither they now often wandered. She smiled as she remembered her own amazement at the sight of the two Englishwomen who had lately arrived there: Mistress Forrest and her maid, Anne Burroughs. With what curiosity the white women and the Indian girl had measured each other, their hair, their eyes, their curious garments! Then she beheld in her fancy her friend, her "brother," so earnest, so brave, who out of opposition always captured victory. She had witnessed how he forced the colonists to labor, had seen the punishment he meted out to those who disobeyed his commands against swearing—that strange offence she could not comprehend—the pouring of cold water in the sleeve of those who uttered oaths, amid the jeers and laughter of their companions. Her lips continued to smile while she thought of Smith, of the gentle words he had ever ready for her, of the interest he ever manifested at all she had to tell him. He had talked to her as she knew he talked to few, of his hopes for this little handful of men who must live and grow, and how, if they two, he and his "little Sister," could bring it about, the English and the Powhatans should forget any grievances against one another and be friends as long as the sky and earth should last. Perhaps, he had said one day, marriages between the English and the Indians might cement this friendship. "Perhaps thou thyself, Matoaka," he had begun, and then had ceased. Now she wondered again, as she had wondered then, if he had perhaps meant himself.

Such a possibility was an exciting one, and she would have been glad to let her mind explore it fully; but her eyes were heavy and the pine needles soft and fragrant, and soon the beaver, who from a hollow beneath the exposed roots of the oak over the stream had been watching her bright eyes, seeing them closed, slipped forth to begin again his work on the dam her feet had flattened out.

Though Nautauquas, returning an hour later from a peaceful mission to a confederated tribe, made scarcely more noise than the beaver, Pocahontas awoke and raised her head and loosening the needles from her hair, sprang up.

"Greetings, Matoaka!" called out her brother. "Thou wert as snugly hidden here as a deer."

"What news, my Brother?" she asked as he sat down and, taking off his moccasins, let his heated feet hang into the stream.

"Evil news it is," he answered gravely, "for the friends of the great Captain."

"What hath befallen my white Brother?" she cried out; "tell me speedily."

"He was sleeping in his boat, I heard, far off from their island. A big bag of the powder they put into their guns lay in the bottom of his canoe, and when by chance a spark from his pipe fell upon it it grew angry and began to spit and burned his flesh till it waked him, and in his agony, he sprang into the river to quench the blaze."

Pocahontas, who had not winced at the thought of the brained Dutchmen, shivered.

"Where is he now?" she asked. "I wish to go to him."

Nautauquas looked at her earnestly as if he would question her, but did not. "They say he is on his way to Jamestown and should reach there on the morrow."

As Pocahontas and Nautauquas returned at sunset to Werowocomoco, the girl stopped at Wansutis's lodge.

"Thou comest for healing herbs for thy white man," exclaimed the old woman before Pocahontas had spoken a word. "I have them here ready for thee," and she thrust a bundle into the astonished maiden's hands. "But," continued the hag, "though they would cure any of our people, they will not have power with the white man's malady save he have faith in them."

Then she went back into the gloom of her lodge and Pocahontas walked away in silence.

It was not Pocahontas whom Wansutis wished to aid, but the white Captain. The old woman had never spoken to him, or of him to others; but she had listened eagerly to all the tales told of his powers. She was sure that he possessed magic knowledge beyond that of her own people, and she waited for the day when she might persuade him to impart some of his medicine to herself. The fact that he was now injured and in danger did not change her opinion. Some medicine was better for certain troubles than for others. Perhaps her herbs in this case would be stronger than his own magic.

Before the night was over Pocahontas had started on her way to Jamestown. She went alone, since somehow she did not wish to chatter with a companion. The thunder storms had cooled the air and softened the earth. It was still early in the morning when she reached the town, now grown to be a settlement of fifty houses. On the wharf she saw men hurrying back and forth to the ship, fastened by stout hawsers to the posts, bearing bundles of bear and fox skins, such as she had seen them purchase from her people, and boxes and trunks up to the deck. One of the latter looked to her strangely like one she had seen in Smith's house, of Cordova leather with a richly wrought iron lock. "Doubtless," she thought, "he is sending it back filled with gifts for the king he speaks so much of."

She hastened towards his house and before she reached it she saw that his bed had been carried outside the door and that he lay upon it, propped up by pillows. She recognized, too, the doctor in the man who was just leaving him. Now in her eagerness she ran the rest of the way and Smith, catching sight of her, waved his hand feebly.

"Alas! my Brother," she cried as she took his hand in hers, and saw how thin it had grown, "alas! how hast thou harmed thyself?"

"Thou hast heard, Matoaka?" he answered, smiling bravely in spite of the pain, "and art come, as thou hast ever come to Jamestown, to bring aid and comfort."

"I have herbs here for thy wound," she replied, taking them out of her pouch. "They will heal it speedily. They are great medicine."

How could he help believe in their power, she had asked herself on her way that morning. What had Wansutis meant?

"I thank thee, little Sister," he answered gently, "for thy loving thought and for the journey thou hast taken. Before thou earnest my heart was low, for I said to myself: how can I go without bidding farewell to Matoaka; yet how can I send a message that will bring her here in time?"

"Go!" she exclaimed. "Where wilt thou go?"

"Home to England. The chirurgeon who hath just left me hath decided only this morn that his skill is not great enough to save my wound, that I must return to the wise men in London to heal me."

"Nay, nay," cried Pocahontas; "thou must not go. Our wise women and our shamans have secrets and wonders thou knowest not of. I will send to them and thy wound shall soon be as clean as the palm of my hand."

"NAY, NAY," CRIED POCAHONTAS, "THOU MUST NOT GO"

"Would that it might be so, little Sister. I have seen in truth strange cures among thy people; and were my ill a fever such as might come to them or the result of an arrow's bite, I would gladly let thy shamans have their will with me. But gunpowder is to them a thing unknown, nor would their remedies avail me aught."

"Then thou wilt go?" she asked in a voice low with despair.

"Aye, Matoaka, I must or else take up my abode speedily yonder," and he pointed to the graveyard. "It is a bitter thing to go now and leave my work unfinished, to know that mine enemies will rejoice—"

"I shall die when thou art gone," she interrupted, kneeling down beside him; "thou hast become like a god to Matoaka, a god strong and wonderful."

"Little Sister! Little Sister!" he repeated as he stroked her hair. Once again there came to him the thought he had harbored before—that perhaps when this child was grown he might claim her as a wife. Now this would never come to pass.

She knelt there still in silence, then she asked, hope and eagerness in her voice: "Thou wilt come back to us?"

"If I may, Matoaka; if I live we shall see each other again."

He did not tell her what was in his mind, that no English Dorothy or Cicely, golden-haired and rosy-cheeked, would ever be as dear to him as he now realized this child of the forest had grown to be.

And then with perfect faith that her "Brother" would bring to pass what he had promised, Pocahontas's spirits rose. She did not try to calculate the weeks and months that should go by before she was to see him again. She seated herself beside him on the ground and listened while he talked to her of all that he was leaving behind and his love and concern for the Colony.

"See, Matoaka," he said, his voice growing stronger in his eagerness, "this town is like unto a child of mine own, so dear is it to me. I have spent sleepless nights and weary days, I have suffered cold and hunger and the contumely of jealous men in its behalf; nay perchance, even death itself. And thou, too, hast shown it great favors till in truth it hath become partly thine own and dear to thee. Now that I must depart, I leave Jamestown to thy care. Wilt thou continue to watch over it, to do all within thy power for its welfare?"

"That will I gladly, my Brother, when thou leavest it like a squaw without her brave. Not a day shall pass that I will not peer through the forests hitherward to see that all be well; mine ears shall harken each night lest harm approach it. 'Jamestown is Pocahontas's friend,' I shall whisper to the north wind, and it will not blow too hard. 'Pocahontas is the friend of Jamestown,' I shall call to the sun that it beat not too fiercely upon it.

'Pocahontas loves Jamestown,' I shall whisper to the river that it eat not too deep into the island's banks, and"—here the half-playful tone changed into one of real earnestness—"I who sit close to Powhatan's heart shall whisper every day in his ear: 'Harm not Jamestown, if thou lovest Matoaka.'"

A look of great relief passed over the wounded man's face. Truly it was a wondrous thing that the expression of a girl's friendship was able to soothe thus his anxieties.

"I thank thee again, little Sister," he said. "And now bid me farewell, for yon come the sailors to bear me to the ship."

Pocahontas sprang up and bending over him, poured forth words of tender Indian farewells. Then, as the bearers approached, she fled towards the gates and into the forest.

John Smith, lying at the prow of the ship, placed there to be nearer the sea as he desired, thought as the ship sailed slowly past the next bend in the river, that he caught sight of a white buckskin skirt between the trees.

CHAPTER XVI

CAPTAIN ARGALL TAKES A PRISONER

And in the three years that had passed since Smith's return to England Pocahontas did not forget the trust he had given her. Many a time had she sent or brought aid to the colonists during the terrible "starving time," and warded off evil from them. When she was powerless to prevent the massacre by Powhatan of Ratcliffe and thirty of his men, she succeeded at least in saving the life of one of his men, a young boy. Henry Spilman, whom she sent to her kindred tribe, the Patowomekes. With them he lived for many years.

But her relations with Jamestown and its people, though most friendly, were no longer as intimate as they had been when Smith was President, and she went there less and less.

One who rejoiced at her home-keeping was Claw-of-the-Eagle. He had hated the white men from the beginning and had done his share to destroy them in the Ratcliffe massacre, though he had never told Pocahontas that he had taken part in it. He was now a brave, tested in courage and endurance in numerous war parties against enemies of his adopted tribe whose honor and advancement he had made his own. The Powhatan himself had praised his deeds in council.

One day Wansutis said to him:

"Son, it is time now that thou shouldst take a squaw into thy wigwam. My hands grow weak and a young squaw will serve thee more swiftly than I. Look about thee, my son, and choose."

Claw-of-the-Eagle had been thinking many moons that the time *had* come to bring home a squaw, but he had no need to look about and choose. He had made his choice, and even though she were the daughter of the great Powhatan, he did not doubt that the werowance would give her to one of his best braves. And so, one evening in taquitock (autumn), when the red glow of the forests was half veiled in the bluish mist that came with the return of soft languid days after frost had painted the trees and ripened the bristly chinquapins and luscious persimmons, Claw-of-the-Eagle took his flute and set forth alone.

Not far from the lodge of Pocahontas he seated himself upon a stone and began to play the plaintive notes with which the Indian lover tells of his longing for the maiden he would make his squaw.

"Dost thou hear that, Pocahontas?" queried Cleopatra, who had peeped out. "It is Claw-of-the-Eagle who pipes for thee. Go forth, Sister, and make glad his heart, for there is none of our braves who can compare with him."

"I will not be his squaw. Go thou thyself if he pleaseth thee so," and Pocahontas would not stir from her tent that evening, though the gentle piping continued until the moon rose.

Yet Claw-of-the-Eagle did not despair. Not only had he won fame as a fighter but as a successful hunter as well. Never did he come back to Wansutis's lodge empty-handed. Though the deer he pursued be never so swift, or the quail never so wary, he always tracked down his quarry. And he meant to succeed in his wooing.

So even when Pocahontas left Werowocomoco to visit her kinsfolk, the Patowomekes, he bided his time and spent his days building a new lodge nearby that of Wansutis, that it might be in readiness for the day when he should bring his squaw to light their first fire beneath the opening under the sky.

Meanwhile affairs in Jamestown had been going from bad to worse. Famine had become an almost permanent visitor there. Sir Thomas Gale had not yet arrived from England and no one was there to govern the Colony with the firm hand of John Smith. At length, however, it was decided in the Council that Captain Argall should set forth towards the Patowomekes tribe and bargain with them for grain.

Japezaws, the chief, received him in a friendly manner.

"Yes, we will sell to thee corn as I sold it to thy great Captain when he first came among us. What news hast thou of him? Will he come again to us? He was a great brave."

Captain Argall answered:

"We have no word from him. Perchance he hath succumbed of his wound;" and then, because he was jealous of Smith's fame among the savages, he added, "England hath so many great braves that we waste little thought on those that are gone. Jamestown hath all but forgot him already."

"There is one amongst us who forgets him not," Japezaws pointed to the valley behind him, "one there is who hath him and his deeds ever on the tongue."

"Who may that be?" asked the Englishman, wondering if the Indian village held captive some countryman of his own long since thought dead.

"It is Pocahontas, his friend, who looks eagerly every moon for his return. She abideth gladly amongst us, for she groweth restless as a young brave, and Werowocomoco hems her in."

Even while Japezaws was speaking a thought flashed through Argall's brain; and while the slaves at Japezaws's command poured forth measure after measure of corn and dried meat, the Englishman was adding to his first vague idea, until when the great load of yellow grain lay heaped before him, his plan was fully laid.

"I wish, Japezaws," he began, as if the idea had just struck him, "that Powhatan, her father, had as great a love for Jamestown as his daughter. He will not even sell to us provisions now, though his storehouse is full to o'erflowing. If we could but make him see that, his gains would be greater than ours. 'Tis a matter of but a few more harvests before we have food and to spare, but where shall he find such copper kettles, such mirrors, such knives of bright steel as we would pay him in exchange for that he hath no need of?"

The old chief's eyes glistened with covetousness.

"I want some shining knives; I want to see a vessel that will not break when my squaws let it fall on a rock. I want some of the marvels ye keep in your lodges."

Argall smiled; the fly had caught the fish for which he angled.

"As soon as a man may hurry to Jamestown and back they shall be thine if—thou wilt do what I ask of thee."

"And what is thy will?" Suspicion had now awakened in the Indian.

"Hearken!" continued Argall. "Thou knowest that Powhatan hath stolen from us sundry arms and keeps in captivity some of our men. If he will make peace with us we need not take our war party through the forests to Werowocomoco, and the lives of many Indians will be spared."

Here Japezaws grunted, but Argall did not appear to notice it.

"If we held a hostage of Powhatan, someone who was dear to him, we could force him to do as we would."

He paused and glanced at the Indian who, whatever he may have thought, betrayed nothing.

"If thou wilt entrust the Princess Pocahontas to us," continued Argall, "she shall be taken to Jamestown and there detained in all gentleness, in the house of a worthy lady, until Powhatan agreeth to our terms and she will be conveyed in safety to her father. And for thee, for thy help in this matter, such presents shall be sent thee as thou hast never seen, such as no one, not even Powhatan, hath yet received."

Japezaws was silent a little. The maiden was his guest, and his people had always upheld the sacred duties of hospitality. But he knew that no harm would befall her. The friendship of the English for her was known to all his tribe and the great affection of her father to this, his favorite daughter. In a day or two she would be ransomed by Powhatan, and for his part in the matter, he, Japezaws, would gain what he so greatly longed to possess. He wasted neither time nor words:

"Meet me here at sunset, and I will bring her to thee."

Claw-of-the-Eagle had not thought to stir away from Wansutis's lodge for many days to come. Food in plenty was stored there and he had need to busy himself with the making of a new bow and arrows. But Wansutis, letting fall the stone with which she was grinding maize, looked up suddenly as if she heard distant voices. The youth, however, heard nothing. Then she said:

"Son, if in truth thy mind is set upon a certain maiden for thy squaw, go seek her at once in the village of the Patowomekes. She hath been there over long."

Claw-of-the-Eagle did not ask for any explanation of his mother's words. He had learned that she seemed to possess some strange knowledge he could not fathom, but which he respected. Therefore, without any discussion, with only a word of farewell, he took his bow and quiver and his wooing pipe and set forth.

As he approached the village of Japezaws at the end of several days' journey, he said to himself:

"Before three days are past I shall return this way with my squaw. No longer will I wait for her to feign deafness to my piping. She shall listen to it and follow me to my lodge."

Knowing that he was among a friendly allied tribe, Claw-of-the-Eagle strode along as openly and as carelessly as he would have done at Werowocomoco or Powhata. Yet suddenly, like a deer that scents a bear, he stood still, his nostrils quivering; then, slipping behind a tree, he notched an arrow to his bow.

"A white man," he thought, long before his eyes caught sight of him.

Concealed by the tree, he waited and watched pass the man he knew was the new English captain, and to his astonishment found that the women who accompanied him were Pocahontas and a squaw of the Patowomekes.

It was the squaw of Japezaws; and it was at his bidding that she was now acting.

"Because thou hast seen as often as thou wilt the lodges of the palefaces," Claw-of-the-Eagle heard her say to Pocahontas, "is it right for thee to marvel that I am eager to witness with mine own eyes such strange ways as are theirs and the marvels the white chief hath stored in the canoe?"

"I do not wonder," laughed Pocahontas; "and in truth I rejoice to go with thee, and with the few words of their tongue that I have not forgotten to ask for thee the questions thou wouldst put to him. I, too, have questions to ask him."

When they had passed the young brave followed them, far off enough that Pocahontas's quick ear might not hear his step that would have been noiseless to the Englishman.

At the bank to which the pinnace was moored he sought cover back of a large boulder, his eyes never moving from the women before him. He watched them go on board, saw the English sailors rise to receive them, and heard the eager outcries of the squaw as she felt of their garments and went about the deck of the little craft, while Pocahontas explained as far as her own knowledge went, the meaning of anchor and sail, of cooking utensils and muskets. He saw Captain Argall open a small chest and hand out presents to the two women, Japezaws's squaw uttering loud cries of delight as beads and gaudy handkerchiefs were placed in her hands.

Claw-of-the-Eagle waited to see what would happen next. After an hour's watching he beheld the two women approach the side of the pinnace nearest the shore, the squaw in front. She sprang to the bank and ran lightly into the forest. Pocahontas had her foot on the gunwale to follow her when Captain Argall took hold of her arm.

"Come with us to Jamestown, Princess," he said; "we will welcome you for a visit."

Pocahontas's anger flared up. Never in her life had she been restrained by force. She wasted no time nor strength in entreaty, but sought to wrench herself away from him. But the Englishman held her firmly but gently, and while she struggled the sailors shoved the boat out into the stream.

Claw-of-the-Eagle rose that he might take better aim and shot an arrow at the Englishman. It hit the astounded captain on his leathern doublet, but did no more than knock the wind out of him.

"Shoot into the trees there," he commanded, still holding on to Pocahontas.

One of the sailors started to aim into the thicket at an unseen enemy, when Claw-of-the-Eagle, realizing that the boat was rapidly swinging out of his range, ran out on to an exposed bluff and notched a second arrow. Before it left the string, however, the bullet from the soldier's musket had hit him in the shoulder. As he fell Pocahontas uttered a cry of horror, for she had seen who her stricken defender was.

CHAPTER XVII

POCAHONTAS LOSES A FRIEND

It was the second night of Pocahontas's captivity. She had suffered no restraint further than that necessary to keep her from jumping overboard. Argall and the sailors treated her with all deference, both from policy and inclination. Yet she was very unhappy and lonely: she had always been so free to go and come that it was almost a physical pain to be imprisoned within the narrow limits of the pinnace. Several times she had tried to evade the vigilance of the sailors; but her cunning, which on shore would have shown her a way to escape, was useless on the unfamiliar boat. Her anger at Japezaws and his squaws flamed up anew every time she dwelt on their treachery. She went over in her mind the punishment she would beg her father to inflict upon them.

"Wait!" she called out; and the sailors wondered what she was saying as she stood there looking over the stern in the direction of the Patowomeke village, her eyes flashing, "wait until Nautauquas brings ye to my father to be tortured!"

Then before she had grown tired planning their fate, her thoughts flew to Claw-of-the-Eagle. Was he lying dead there in the forest? What a playmate and companion he had always been, she thought; how brave, how strong! Yet now he must be dead or surely he had managed to follow her.

By nightfall the boat was anchored in the centre of the stream, which here widened out into a small bay. Captain Argall, who had not known what to make of Claw-of-the-Eagle's attack, did not feel certain that Japezaws had not played him false. He had therefore made all speed possible the first night and the following day. Now his wearied men needed rest and, as no sign of pursuit appeared, he had granted them leave to sleep. Only one sailor in the bow was left on watch, but he, too, drowsed, to wake up with a start, when finding all well, he dropped off to sleep again.

Pocahontas lay alone in the stem, her head pillowed on a roll of sail cloth that brought it up to the level of the gunwale. Argall had done everything he could to make her comfortable and never even spoke to her except hat in hand and bowing low. Now she, too, had fallen asleep, her eyes wet with the tears she would not shed during the daylight. She dreamed she was again at Werowocomoco and that she had just risen from her sleeping-mat to run out into the moonlight as she so often did.

Suddenly a faint, faint sound half wakened her, a sound scarcely louder than the lapping of the water against the sides which had lulled her to sleep. She opened her eyes but did not move, and waited, tense with excitement. A fish flopped out of the water, then all was silent again and she closed her heavy eyes once more. Then it came again, not louder than the wind in the aspen trees on shore:

"Pocahontas!"

Raising herself to her elbow with a motion as quiet as a cat's, she peered into the dark water over the stern. A hand came up from the darkness and clasped her wrist. She needed no great light upon the features of the face below to know whose it was.

"Claw-of-the-Eagle," she whispered, "is it thou? I thought the white man's gun had killed thee, and I have been mourning for thee."

"I lay dead for an hour," he answered as he lifted himself up in the water and hung with both hands to the sides of the boat. "But it was well that I was wounded on the shoulder and not on the leg. The stiffness made me slow, like a bear that has been hurt in a trap. But I bound mud on the wound with my leggings and I have followed close behind thee along the shore all the way."

"I knew thou wouldst come after me if thou wert not killed," she whispered.

"Yea, I have come for thee, Pocahontas," and there was manly decision now in the youth's voice. "Waste no time. Drop down here beside me as quietly as if thou wert stalking a deer. We will swim under water until we are beyond reach of the white men's dull ears and before three days are passed we shall be at Powhata, where thy father now abideth."

The thought of all home meant made Pocahontas pause: the kindly interest of all her tribe in everything she did; the affection of her father and brothers; the haunts in the forest and on the river; the freedom of her daily existence. Here was her chance to return to them. If she did not take it, what lay ahead of her? A terror of the unknown overcame her for the first time. The knowledge that an old and tried friend was near was as grateful as a light shining before one on a dark night. Yet she answered:

"I can not go with thee, Claw-of-the-Eagle."

The young brave uttered a low murmur of astonishment.

"Dost thou not know," he asked, "that Japezaws hath betrayed thee; that thou art to be kept captive in Jamestown in order to force The Powhatan to do whatever the English desire of him?"

"Yes, I know. Captain Argall hath told me all."

"And yet thou dost hesitate? Art thou, the daughter of a mighty werowance, *afraid* to try to escape?"

She did not deign to reply to such a charge, but whispered instead:

"Hadst thou come last night I should have harkened to thee only too gladly. In truth, I had determined to escape myself this night, no matter what the difficulties might be. Pocahontas beareth a knife and knoweth how to use it. But to-day I have come to think otherwise, for there have been long hours in which to think. Thou knowest that captivity is as wearisome to me as to a wild dove; yet as I sat here alone with naught to do, I followed a trail in my mind that led to Jamestown, and so I am minded to go thither."

"But why?" asked Claw-of-the-Eagle.

"Because by going I believe I can serve both our nation and the English. My Brother, John Smith, said we must be friends, and I promised him e'er he left to watch ever over the welfare of his people. My father loveth me so much that in order to free me I think he will do as the English wish, and so I will go with Captain Argall that the strife may cease between them and us. But," and here her voice rose so that Claw-of-the-Eagle had to remind her of their danger by a pressure on the hand, "but I will not intercede for that traitor Japezaws and his crafty squaw. My father may wreak vengeance on them when he will."

Her voice, low as it was, had risen in her emotion, and the boy's keen hearing had caught the movement of a man's foot on the wooden deck. They kept still, breathless, for a moment; then as all was still again, Claw-of-the-Eagle asked sadly, in a tone that mourned as wind through the pine trees:

"Then thou wilt not come with me? I had built a lodge for thee, Matoaka, with a smoke hole wide enough to let in the whole moon thou lovest. My arrows had killed young deer and turkeys and I had smoked and hung meat for thee to last through all popanow (winter). A young maid is lonely till she follows her brave—all this I came to the village of Japezaws to pipe to thee. Now I have run wounded through the forests and swum the black stream to tell it to thee, and thou bidst me turn back alone. But if thou hast no wish to enter Claw-of-the-Eagle's lodge let him at least escort thee safely to the wigwam of thy father."

"I thank thee, Claw-of-the-Eagle, for all thou hast done," she whispered, "and all thou wouldst do for me. There is no braver warrior in the thirty tribes and no better hunter since Michabo. But I have listened to my manitou and he hath said to me, 'Remember the word thou gavest to thy white Brother.'"

Claw-of-the-Eagle knew that it was useless to plead and yet he pleaded: "Come back with me, Matoaka; what are the white men to thee and me?"

But she whispered: "Go, Claw-of-the-Eagle, go quickly ere the sailors awake. Hasten back to old Wansutis that she may bind up thy wound, and to Powhatan and tell him that he must buy Pocahontas's freedom from the English by returning their men he holdeth prisoners."

While she was still speaking the young brave's mind was working rapidly. At first the respect he owed her as the daughter of the great werowance was uppermost and he thought he must needs do her bidding and leave her. Little by little, however, he began to think of her as a young maiden, strong and courageous, but not so strong as a man, who now stood in need of the help of a brave. He hated the English more than ever, and Pocahontas's promise to aid them seemed to him only a girlish foolishness. Let them all perish on their island or return across the sea whence they had come. Why should she go with them? Why should he let her go? Who knew what treatment she would receive away from her own people? If he should rescue her and bring her back to her father, would he not thus win great favor in the eyes of Powhatan, who would not refuse her to him as his squaw? If she would not come willingly, he would carry her off against her will for her good.

Rescue Pocahontas! And in addition—kill the hated white men! Had they not wounded him and carried her off? There were not many of them and they were all asleep. While he and Pocahontas had talked he had pulled himself out of the water and thrown his legs over the stern. Now he rose and whispered:

"Before I go I would know what their canoe is like. Be not afeared for me; there is no danger, only do not stir."

She wished to remonstrate with him, but he was already a few paces ahead of her, treading as lightly as if the deck were gravel that would roll about and betray him with its noise, and she did not dare call out to him. She saw him draw near to a sleeping sailor and stoop; but it was too dark for her to see that he had placed his hand over the man's mouth and with the knife in his other hand, had stabbed him to the heart.

The sailor's dying struggles were noiseless and when they were over Claw-of-the-Eagle moved softly on to the next.

There was something sinister to Pocahontas in the silence; she began to divine that it was not mere curiosity which was keeping Claw-of-the-Eagle, and yet she dared not go in search of him.

The second victim was despatched as easily as the first, and the third, though he awoke before the blow was struck, was unable to avert it. The young brave, whose lust for slaughter increased as he went on, felt about for Captain Argall. Already the dawn was coming, and he could distinguish the forms of the four other men. He bent over one of them; his hand, burning with the fever from his wound and excitement, touched the cheek of the man instead of the mouth. The sailor cried out instantaneously even before he was awake; and Claw-of-the-Eagle, realizing in a second that his game was up, slashed out with his knife at him in passing as he ran for the stern.

He could have leapt overboard more easily, but though he had failed to kill all his enemies, he meant to rescue Pocahontas. He dashed towards her, followed by the sailor. Argall and the two others of the crew, roused at the outcry, were at their heels. Claw-of-the-Eagle caught Pocahontas in his arms and before she knew what was happening, he had sprung with her into the river.

The sailor, who had been but slightly wounded by the young brave's knife, had seized his musket as he ran. His forebears had been outlaws with Robin Hood, skilful archers, and bowmen with Henry V at Agincourt, whose arrows never failed to find French marks. The same keen eye and strong arm were his with a musket.

"Do not shoot. Mark!" called out Argall breathlessly. He did not know what had happened prior to his own awakening, though his feet had stumbled over the dead bodies of his men. "The Indian princess is there in the water. Shoot not, for the love of heaven, or we'll have all the red hordes of America on top of Jamestown!"

Mark, however, had already made out the two figures in the water so close together that Argall's older eyes thought them but one. And just as Claw-of-the-Eagle, hampered by his wounded shoulder, was about to sink below the surface of the river to swim under water, Mark took aim. The bullet hit the top of the head, gashing the skin about the scalp-lock, but did not penetrate very deeply.

"DO NOT SHOOT, MARK!"

Pocahontas saw that he was not badly wounded; but the blood running down his face and into his mouth and nose made it impossible for him to breathe deeply enough to swim under water. His weakness from his other wound, too, made his motions slower. Before he would be able to put a safe distance between him and the pinnace the sailor would have fired again.

But he would not fire at her—the thought flashed through her brain!

With a few rapid strokes she had reached the brave and flung her arm under his wounded shoulder, bearing him up.

"Now, Claw-of-the-Eagle," she cried, "let us make for the shore. They will not dare fire at me."

And Argall and his men watched their hostage and the murderer of their companions making their escape, while they seemed powerless to prevent it. Though Claw-of-the-Eagle's strokes grew slower and slower, Pocahontas's strength was aiding him. Once on shore, the Englishmen knew that even though delayed by his wound, the two could hide so that no white man could find them. Besides, it was likely that other Indians might be lurking in the forest.

"Fooled! Fooled!" cried out Argall, hitting one fist against the other in his disappointment.

But Mark was not one who willingly gave up a chase he had begun. He saw that the two had reached a willow tree with roots that lay twisted about each other across the surface of the river. For one second the youth and maiden, close together, hung on to this natural shelf, gaining strength to pull themselves up on to the ground. He realized how disastrous it would be to injure the daughter of the Powhatan. Nevertheless, he determined to take a chance.

To the horror of his captain, he took careful aim and fired. This time the bullet found its mark—it hit the young brave in the back of his head and penetrated the brain.

In horror Pocahontas tried to catch him in her arms before he sank heavily, with no sound, out of sight. Gone! so quickly! Dead! The boy who had been her friend, who had tried to save her!

She could not weep as she floated along with no conscious movement. Then slowly she turned and swam back towards the pinnace, the sailors wondering if she was in truth returning to them. She let herself be helped over the side by Captain Argall.

"I will go with thee to Jamestown, now," was all that she said. She gave no explanation of what had happened and refused to answer their questions, or to tell them why she had chosen to go with them when she might have regained her freedom.

They had hoisted the anchor and started off after laying their dead comrades together. The sun was rising but the air was still chill and the sailors brought their dry coats to Pocahontas to throw over her and placed food before her. She would not touch it nor turn her face away from the river behind her.

As they began to sail slowly down the stream she leaned back over the gunwale and beheld, borne by a swift eddy, the body of Claw-of-the-Eagle float by her. She rose to her feet, the sunbeams falling upon her face and her uplifted arms, and she sang aloud a song of death as her tribe sang it while the river hurried with its burden seawards.

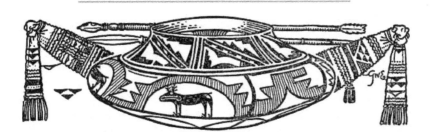

CHAPTER XVIII

A BAPTISM IN JAMESTOWN

Very unhappy was Pocahontas the rest of the voyage to Jamestown. Claw-of-the-Eagle had been dear to her as a brother, and she sorrowed for him greatly. It was forlorn to be away thus from her own people and among those whose ways and tongue were strange to her; and she longed for Nautauquas, whom she had not seen for several moons.

News of their coming had outrun them, and all of Jamestown was at the wharf to greet them. Captain Argall stepped ashore and explained that he had brought generous stores and what was of far greater value, the daughter of Powhatan. Sir Thomas Dale, in all the bravery of his best purple doublet and new bright Cordova leather boots, came forward and doffing his plumed hat, said:

"Welcome, Princess, and be not angry with us if we in all courtesy constrain thee to abide with us awhile. Let it not irk thee to visit us again, to stay for a few days with those who have been thy debtors since the time thou didst save the life of Captain Smith."

Pocahontas, whose anger had been rising at the treachery practised on her by Japezaws and Argall, had intended to show in her manner how she resented it; but the name of Captain Smith disarmed her. She recalled her white Brother's parting words to her.

She would befriend his colony, as she had ever done. So she smiled at Sir Thomas and spoke to those about whom she knew and let them show her the way to the house that they chose for her use, a few paces from the Governor's. Mistress Lettice, the wife of one of the gentlemen, who was to occupy it with her, laid out some of her own garments in case the Indian maiden should care to change; and Pocahontas, forgetting the dangers and sadness of the past days, laughed with amusement as she tried on farthingale and wide skirt.

"They are sending messengers to thy father. King Powhatan," the Englishwoman said as she showed Pocahontas how to adjust a starched ruff that scratched her neck so that she made a grimace. "They will tell him that thou art here, and then surely in his anxiety to see thee again, he will grant what Sir Thomas desires: that he deliver up our men and the arms he hath taken and give us three hundred quarters of corn. Perchance thou wouldst like to send some word of thine own to thy father. If so be, there is an Indian boy who hath brought fish to trade, and he can bear it for thee."

"Bring him to me, I pray thee," said Pocahontas, speaking slowly the unaccustomed English words.

She was looking at herself in the ebony-framed mirror that hung opposite the door, much interested in her strange appearance, when the Indian boy entered, following Mistress Lettice. She saw his face in the glass and recognized him as the son of a Powhatan chief. She turned and faced him, but knew that he did not recognize her. He looked no further than her clothes and so believed her an Englishwoman. It was a rare amusement, she thought, and she watched him eagerly to see his surprise when he should find out his mistake. She was well rewarded by his puzzled and astonished expression when she called out to him:

"Little Squirrel!" When she herself had stopped laughing, she added: "Take this sad message to old Wansutis. Tell her that her son, Claw-of-the-Eagle, hath met his death bravely and that Pocahontas mourns him with her."

Then she dismissed the boy. As he walked away she remembered that she desired him to bear also a special word to Nautauquas, so she started to run and call him back. But the unaccustomed weight of her clothes and shoes prevented her and she began to pull them off her even before she reached the house, crying out:

"Nay, I will not prison myself thus; give me back mine own garments," and she breathed deep breaths of satisfaction when she had resumed them.

Had the manner of her coming to Jamestown been otherwise, with no treachery and no compulsion which hurt her pride, Pocahontas would have much enjoyed her stay and a closer view of the ways of the English. As it was, she was restlessly awaiting the message her father would return to the demands of the colonists. The next day the messengers came back, bringing with them the Englishmen who had been held captive by Powhatan and some of the arms. The werowance promised, they reported, that when his daughter was restored to him he would give the corn which the white men asked for.

This answer did not satisfy the Council, and day by day there were parleyings in which the white men and the red men sought to constrain or evade each other. Each side recognized the value of Pocahontas as a hostage. She was not now unhappy. Even if the colonists had not done their best to requite with kindness all the care she had manifested for their welfare, policy would have led them to treat her with every consideration. She was made welcome everywhere, and she went from the guard house to that of the Governor, asking questions, eager to learn all details, from the way to fire off a musket to the heating of the sealing wax and the making of a great red seal which Master John Rolfe, Secretary and Recorder General of the Colony, affixed to all the documents sent to the Company in London.

He explained everything to her, taking pains to choose the simplest words, because he found a keen pleasure in watching her dark eyes brighten when she began to comprehend something which had puzzled her, and because her laughter and quick coming and going in the masculine atmosphere of the council room was a most agreeable change from its usual dull calm. He was a widower and, though he had got over the sadness of the loss of his wife, he still missed a woman's companionship. So he was nothing loath to follow when Pocahontas commanded one day:

"Come with me about the town and answer more of my questions. I have stored away as many as a squirrel stores nuts for popanow—what keeps the ship from floating with the tide down to the great water? Why doth that man sit with his legs before him?"—and she pointed to a carpenter who had been imprisoned in the stocks in punishment for theft—"And why?"—
...

And Rolfe found himself kept as busy as Mr. Squirrel himself in cracking her questions for her.

She soon got over her awe of the white men, judging, now that she had a closer view of them, that they were in many ways like her own people. And seeing that her lightheartedness was pleasant to them, she teased and joked with them.

"Wilt thou eat a persimmon?" she asked Rolfe, smiling at the trap she was laying as she stood on tiptoe to pick one from a branch above her. And Rolfe bit into the golden fruit, not knowing that the persimmon till ripened by frost is for the eye only. She laughed with glee as she saw his mouth all puckered up until he believed it would never unpucker again.

"I'll pay thee for this some day," he threatened in mock anger as soon as he could speak; but she only laughed the more.

One of the reasons that Pocahontas was content to remain in Jamestown was that she hoped to get news of Captain Smith's return. Every day she would ask, sometimes Mistress Lettice, sometimes Sir Thomas Dale, or anyone with whom she spoke:

"When cometh back the Captain? I am longing to see my Brother."

And one told her one thing, one another, some lying because it was easier; some from sheer ignorance said they had heard that John Smith had gone back to fight the Turks; that he grew fat and lazy in his English home; that he was exploring further up the coast; that he might be expected at Jamestown with the next ship. And Pocahontas, believing those who said the last because she wished this to be the truth, was not unhappy to wait among strangers that she might be the first to welcome him.

The spot in the town which most excited her curiosity was the church. The colonists had now replaced the first rude hut by a substantial building with a tower. The bells that called Jamestown to daily prayers had a weird fascination for the Indian girl. They seemed to speak a language she could not understand. Nor could she understand the ceremony which she observed, wide-eyed, of the kneeling men and women and the white-robed clergyman who stretched out his arms over them.

"What doth it signify?" she queried; and Rolfe, remembering that the conversion of the heathen was one of the reasons given by Europe for sending colonies to the New World, tried to explain the mysteries of his faith to her. But he found it too difficult a task, and besought the Reverend Thomas Alexander Whitaker to undertake it in his stead.

This the zealous and gentle minister of the Gospel gladly consented to do. Here was the great opportunity he had desired since his coming to Virginia—to make an Indian convert so notable that this conversion might bring others in its train. Moreover the maiden herself interested him. But it was not so easy to go about it. Pocahontas's knowledge of English did not extend beyond the simplest expressions; and he found it necessary to translate the long and abstruse theological dogmas into familiar terms. He had almost despaired of making her comprehend until he recalled how his Master had taught in parables. So he retold the incidents of His life in stories which held the Indian maiden spellbound. He showed her pictures in heavy leathern-bound volumes, and tried with less success to explain the meaning of the daily religious services he conducted in the church.

"Why do ye put always flowers on that table?" she asked, pointing to the vases on the altar which the Governor bade keep always filled with fresh blossoms as long as the forests and river bank could supply them. "What good hath thy god of them?"

"Dost thou not take delight in the sunshine. Princess?" replied the priest as they sat in the cool shade of the darkened church looking out through the open door at waving green branches and the river beyond. "I have beheld thee lift up thine arms on a fair day when the swift white clouds moved across the blue heavens as if thou wouldst embrace the whole wide earth. Why dost thou take pleasure in such things?"

"Because," hesitated the maiden, seeking for a reason, "because they make me happy."

"Because," he added, "they are beautiful. And God who created all this beauty rejoiceth too in it—in green fields and noble trees, in lovely maidens, strong men and happy children. Therefore, in token thereof, we place beautiful flowers upon His table."

"And delighteth he not in incantations of shamans and jossakeed (inspired prophets) and in self-torture?" she queried.

"Nay," he answered; "such things are of the Devil; our God is love. Ponder upon the difference."

And Pocahontas did think much of what he told her. Her spirit was maturing in this new atmosphere like a quick-growing vine climbing higher each day. Dr. Whitaker's own fatherly kindness to her and to all the colony became for her the symbol of the tenderness of the God of whom he taught her. Then, too, this strange new deity was the god of her Brother, John Smith; and whatever in any way was dear to him she wanted to make her own.

For weeks the instruction continued and at last Dr. Whitaker told Sir Thomas Dale that he believed the Indian princess was now sufficiently impressed with the teachings of Christianity to be baptized. So Sir Thomas, meeting her one afternoon as she stood by the wharf watching men unload a ship but newly arrived from England, began:

"Good even, Princess, I rejoice at the news Dr. Whitaker hath even now imparted to me, that he hath instructed thee fully in the teachings of our blessed faith, and that thou hast shown wisdom and comprehension. The time hath therefore arrived for thee to bear witness before man to the truth and to accept the blessed sacrament of baptism at his hands and to swear publicly that thou wilt have naught more to do with the heathen gods whom thy people ignorantly worship."

"I will not give them up," Pocahontas cried out in anger such as she had not shown for many a day; and to Sir Thomas's amazement, she turned her back upon his presence and sped, swift as a fawn, into the thicket which still covered a portion of the island.

There she lay upon the ground, panting with emotion and passionately going over her arguments: "Why should I forsake the Okee of my fathers? Why should I hate what my brothers serve? Why should I prefer this god of the strangers?"

She did not know that a sudden attack of homesickness was the principal cause of this outburst. She was longing to sit at her father's knee, to hunt with Nautauquas; and she wondered if they had ceased to care for her that they left her to stay among the strangers.

Here, at sunset, Dr. Whitaker, set upon her track by the startled Sir Thomas, found her and seating himself beside her, he talked to her gently, not finding fault with her loyalty to her people and their beliefs, but explaining how they had never had the chance to hear what she was being taught, and how by acknowledging the Christians' God, she might lead those she loved to do the same and to benefit by His great gifts.

Not in one day did the clergyman convince her; but by the time April had come Pocahontas eagerly consented to her baptism. Clothed by Mistress Lettice in a simple white gown free from ruff and farthingale, with her long black hair hanging down her back, Pocahontas walked to the little church filled with all the inhabitants and a few Indians from the mainland who wondered what it all meant; and while the bells rang softly in the soft spring air, Pocahontas, the first of her race, was baptized into the Christian faith, with the new name of Rebecca.

CHAPTER XIX

JOHN ROLFE

To John Rolfe and to all who observed closely the Lady Rebecca—as she was now called—it seemed as if the little Indian maiden had put on a new womanly dignity since her baptism. And to John Rolfe in special she grew more lovely every day. He spent much time with her, strolling all over Jamestown island and even the mainland. In the woods she taught him as much as he taught her in the town: to observe the habits of the wild animals and to find his way through a trackless forest. Often they would go in a boat to catch fish or to dig for oysters in the Indian fashion.

At times Rolfe was very happy, and at other moments perplexed and cast down. It was joy for him to be in the company of one who made him feel how splendid a thing was life and how full of interest and beauty the woods, fields and river. Yet when the thought of marriage came to him he remembered the difficulties in the way. First, she was, though called a princess, only the child of a cruel savage chief and one accustomed to savage ways. Why should he, an English gentleman, choose her instead of a woman of his own race brought up in the manner of his people?

Then, even if he were willing, it was unlikely that Powhatan would consent to let his daughter wed a white man or the Governor on his side allow it. So he pondered; but no matter what the obstacles in his way, he came back again and again to his determination to win Pocahontas's love and to marry her. Now that she had become a Christian, there was one less barrier between them.

Rolfe believed that his feelings for Pocahontas had gone unnoticed by anyone, but Mistress Lettice, who had grown very fond of the Indian maiden confided to her especial care, was far from blind in anything that concerned her charge. Moreover, she had heard enough of the discussions which went on in the Council to know that such a marriage would be approved, since it would secure to the Colony the valuable friendship of Powhatan. But she was also aware of an obstacle which might prevent its coming to pass. This knowledge of hers she was determined to share.

One day she invited certain members of the Council to her house to drink a cask of sack her brother in London had sent her by the last ship. She had baked cake, also, and so excellent was its taste after the weariness of plain baker's bread, that many of her guests sighed at the remembrance of their womanless households; and those who had wives behind in England determined to send for them without further delay.

"But what I have to say, your Worships," she continued when she had ceased serving and had settled down in a highbacked chair to rest, "is that the Lady Rebecca will never wed another while she harboureth the thought of Captain Smith's return."

"What! did he teach her to love him?" exclaimed one who would gladly have listened to any ill of Smith.

"Nay, if ye should even question her thus she would not know how to reply. She thinketh and speaketh of him constantly and in her thoughts he standeth midway between a god and an elder brother, even as she doth call him. All the knowledge she acquireth is learned because she believeth he would wish it and will be glad to know that she is no longer the ignorant child of the woods as he first saw her. She wished even to delay her baptism because she expecteth him by every ship, and this I know full well—she will marry no man until she hath speech with Captain Smith or," here she paused significantly, "she believeth him to be dead."

She paused again to let her words sink in. Mistress Lettice wished no harm to Pocahontas. Indeed she loved her dearly and desired above all things to see her happy. And she believed that Rolfe as her husband would make her happy. Smith, if not indeed dead, was not likely to return to Jamestown, and therefore he might better be dead as far as Pocahontas was concerned, she thought. The worthy dame had picked her audience, which was composed chiefly of men who were well known to be enemies of Smith, who would not hold back from a slight untruth when they felt sure that it would help to secure safety from Indian attacks, which were proving so disastrous to their small community.

"We are mightily amazed at thy words. Mistress Lettice," said one of her guests at last; "and in truth it hath taken thy woman's eyes to see what was going on under our very noses and thy woman's tongue to show us the importance of Master Rolfe's courtship to the welfare of the Colony. If so small a thing as what thou hast suggested is all that stands between us and the confirmation of this marriage, why, that is as easily disposed of as this flagon of thy brother's sack which I drink to thy health."

He put the emptied cup upon the table and the company rose to go, now that both business and pleasure were finished. They did not need much talk about what they intended to do.

As they were bidding Mistress Lettice farewell, with many compliments on her housewifery and her zeal for the settlement, Pocahontas appeared at the door. She had been, as Mistress Lettice well knew, away with Rolfe, showing him how her people planted tobacco, since he had become much interested in this weed—being the first in the Colony to grow it—and had expressed what seemed to his neighbors ridiculous hopes of future wealth to be derived from the sale of tobacco in England.

Pocahontas looked about her with eagerness, and while the men doffed their hats, she asked:

"What hath happened, sirs, that so many come to visit us at one time? It is like our councils when the old chiefs debate about the council fires."

No one was anxious to be the first to answer, but since some reply was necessary, the councilor who had testified to Mistress Lettice's insight said slowly and solemnly:

"We have come. Princess, to condole with thee at the death of thy friend, Captain John Smith."

"Dead!" cried Pocahontas. "He is dead?"

And the men, who wished not to burden their consciences with a spoken lie, all nodded assent. They thought to see the girl burst into tears or run away, as they had more than once seen her do when she was displeased; but instead she stood still, her face as motionless as a statue's. They were glad to slip away with muttered words of sympathy.

Nor when they were gone did Mistress Lettice's curious and affectionate eyes witness any sign of sorrow.

"I own myself wrong," she said that night to her husband; "she careth naught for the Captain. I wept all day last Michaelmas when my old dog died."

But Mistress Lettice did not hear the door unlatched that night, nor the moccasined feet of Pocahontas as they sped through the street down to a quiet spot on the river bank whither she often went. The maiden's heart was so full that under a roof she felt it would burst. And until dawn she stood on the shore, her face turned eastward towards the sea across which he had sailed away, bewailing her "Brother" in the manner of her people, now calling to Okee to guide him to the happy hunting grounds, and now praying God to bear his soul to the Christian heaven.

John Rolfe found nothing amiss with Pocahontas when he saw her next day, nor did any of the conspirators tell him of the false news that they had communicated to Lady Rebecca or their interest in his wooing.

And his wooing was very gentle and wonderful to Pocahontas. No Indian lover, she knew, ever won his squaw in this way. She listened to his words with amazement when he told her that he wanted her to be his wife, to make a home for him in this new land. When she gave him her word she felt much as if she were the very heroine of one of the tales she had listened to so often about the lodge fire, a deer perhaps that was to be magically transformed into human shape, or a bird on whom the spirits had bestowed speech—so immeasurably superior did the English still appear to her.

It was some weeks later that Sir Thomas Dale, grown impatient for a settlement of their differences with Powhatan, decided to go to Werowocomoco and take Pocahontas with him to act as peacemaker. With them, on Argall's ship, went John Rolfe and Master Sparkes and one hundred and fifty men.

When they tried to land at a village near Werowocomoco the Indians were very arrogant and opposed their passage. In return the English fired upon them and when the terrified savages ran into the forest to escape the white men's weapons, the victors burned all the lodges of the town and wantonly spoiled the corn stacked up in a storehouse.

Pocahontas, who was sorrowful at the enmity between those she loved, besought Sir Thomas:

"Let me go among my people. They will harken to me and I will hasten to my father, and when he beholdeth me once more he will deny me nothing. And it is a long time since I have looked upon his face," she pleaded.

But Sir Thomas refused. He was not minded to lose this valuable hostage; even though Pocahontas might be eager to return, he was sure that the old chieftain would never let her leave him.

"Prithee, then," she suggested sadly, "send messengers in my name, saying that ye will abstain from further fighting for a night and day. If the messengers bear this feather of mine," here she took a white eagle's feather from her headband, "they may pass in safety where they will." As they were leaving she charged them: "And beg of my father to send my brothers to see me, since I may not go to them."

Now that she was so near home again she was homesick for the sight of some member of her family that she had not seen for many moons. Her father would not come, she felt sure, because he would not wish to treat with the white men in person. She waited anxiously, her eyes and ears strained for the sound of the messengers returning.

An hour or so later she beheld in the distance two tall figures approaching, and she sprang ashore from the boat, crying:

"Nautauquas! Catanaugh!" as her two brothers hurried to meet her.

"Is it indeed our little Matoaka?" asked Nautauquas, "and unharmed and well?"

He looked at her critically, as if seeking to discover some great change in her.

"We feared we knew not what evil medicine they might have used against thee, little Snow Feather. How have they dealt with thee in thy captivity?"

"But fear no longer," cried Catanaugh, whose glance was fixed upon the canoe of the palefaces; "we shall rescue thee now if we have to kill every one of them yonder to get thee free."

"Nay, my brothers," said Pocahontas, laying her hand gently on his sinewy arm, "they are my friends, and they have treated me well. Look! am I wasted with starvation or broken with torture? Harm them not. I am come to plead with our father to make peace with them. It is as if yon tree should plead with the sky and the earth not to quarrel, since both are dear to it. The English are a great nation. Let us be friends with them."

"Have they bewitched thee, Matoaka?" asked Catanaugh sternly. "Hast thou forgot thy father's lodge now that thou hast dwelt among these strangers?"

"Nay, Brother, but...."

Nautauquas was quick to notice Pocahontas's confusion and the blush that stole over her soft dark cheek.

"I think," he said, smiling at her, "that our little Sister hath a story to tell us. Let us sit here beneath the trees, as we so often sat when we were wearied hunting, and listen to her words."

It was not easy at first for Pocahontas to explain how it had come about. But as she sat there on the warm brown pine needles, snuggled closely against Nautauquas's shoulder, she found courage to tell of the strong, fine Englishman who had taught her so much, and how one day he had asked her to become his squaw after the manner of the white people. She told them also how Sir Thomas Dale, the Governor, had willingly given his consent.

"Believe ye not," she concluded, looking eagerly first at one and then the other of her brothers, "that our father will make peace for my sake with the nation to which my brave belongeth?"

Catanaugh said nothing, but Nautauquas laid his hand on his sister's arm and looked her in the eyes searchingly:

"Art thou happy?"

"Yea, Brother, very happy. He is dear to me because I know him and because I know him not. Thou surely hast not forgotten how Matoaka ever longed for what lay unknown beyond her."

"Hath thy manitou spoken?" questioned Nautauquas again.

"The God of the Christians is my god now," she answered.

"So should it be," said Nautauquas, although Catanaugh scowled; "a woman must worship the spirits to which her brave prayeth. Then all is well with thee?"

"All if my father will but make peace. I would I might go to see him. Doth he love me still?" she asked wistfully.

"He saith," answered Nautauquas, "that he loveth thee as his life and, though he hath many children, that he delighteth in none so much as in thee."

Pocahontas sighed half sadly, half happily. "Bear to him my loving greetings. Brother," she said, "and say to him that Matoaka's thoughts go to him each day, even as the tide cometh up the river from the sea."

"He hath agreed," said Catanaugh, "to a truce until taquitock (fall of the leaf) if the English will send important hostages to him, whom he may hold as they hold thee."

"And Cleopatra and our other sisters and old Wansutis, how is it with them all, and...." and Pocahontas strung the names of most of the inhabitants of Werowocomoco together in her enquiries. She listened to all the news they had to tell her of the great deeds accomplished by the young braves and the wise speeches made by the old chiefs in council, of the harvest dances, of the losses on the warpath, and of old Wansutis, who had grown more strange and more silent since Claw-of-the-Eagle's death. Then Pocahontas told them of the manner of his going; and Catanaugh's eyes flashed as he heard of the three palefaces his friend had slain.

They had not noticed how long they had sat there chatting until they saw Sir Thomas himself coming down from the ship, accompanied by Rolfe and Master Sparkes.

"These two, Princess," he said, "will be the hostages we send to thy father; and thy brothers will remain with us."

The two Indians looked at the white men keenly. From the glance their sister gave Rolfe they knew he must be her affianced husband. And Rolfe looked with the same curiosity at his future brothers-in-law. They were tall like their father, strong and well-built, men such as other men liked to look at, no matter what their color might be. But it was Nautauquas in particular that pleased him. He recalled that John Smith had said of him that he was "the most manliest, comliest, boldest spirit I ever saw in a savage."

After they had conversed for a little, Rolfe and Sparkes, accompanied by certain Indians to whom Nautauquas confided them, set out on their way to Werowocomoco. They did not fear that harm would come to them, but they begrudged the time they must spend away from the colony. On their arrival Powhatan, who was still angry with the English, refused to see them, so Opechanchanough entertained them and promised to intercede with his brother for them. Nautauquas's messenger had brought him the news of Rolfe's relation to his niece.

In the meantime the truce was extended until the autumn and the Englishmen were sent back to Jamestown. Nautauquas and Catanaugh had enjoyed their time on the island among the palefaces, Catanaugh being interested only in the fort and its guns and in the ship, and Nautauquas, not only in these, but in talking as well as he could with the colonists. He and Pocahontas again went hunting together on the mainland, for the Governor allowed them full liberty to come and go as they pleased, feeling sure that Nautauquas would keep his word not to leave Jamestown until the Powhatan sent back Rolfe and Sparkes.

And the day that these returned the two braves set off to join their father at Orapaks.

CHAPTER XX

THE WEDDING

Everyone in Jamestown was astir early one April morning in 1614. The soldiers and the few children of the settlement, impressed with the importance of their errand, had gone into the woods to cut large sprays of wild azalea and magnolia to deck the church.

Sir Thomas Dale, and in truth all the cavaliers of the town, had seen that their best costumes were in order, sighing at the moth holes in precious cloth doublets and the rents in Flemish lace collars and cuffs, yet satisfied on the whole with their holiday appearance. The few women of the Colony, Mistress Easton, Mistress Horton, Elizabeth Parsons and others, had of course prepared their garments many days before. It was not often they had an excuse for decking themselves in the finery they had packed with such care and misgivings back in their English homes; and this was an occasion such as no one in the world had ever before participated in. Here was an English gentleman of old lineage who was to wed the daughter of a great heathen ruler, one in whose power it lay to help or hinder the progress of this first permanent English colony in the New World. In addition to making themselves as gay as possible, they had prepared a wedding breakfast to be served to the gentry at the Governor's house, and the Governor had provided that meat and other viands and ale should be distributed from the general store to the soldiers and laborers and the Indians, their guests.

The guard at the fort was kept busy admitting the Indians and bidding them lay aside their bows, hatchets or knives; though in truth no one that day looked for any hostile act, since Powhatan's consent to his daughter's marriage had put an end to the enmity between them.

He himself had not come to the ceremony. He was not minded to set his foot upon any land other than his own, but he had sent as his representative Pocahontas's uncle, Opechisco, and many messages of affection to "his dearest daughter." The elderly werowance wore all the ceremonial robes of his tribe: a headdress of feathers, leggings and girdle and a long deerskin mantle heavily embroidered in beads of shell. With him came Nautauquaus and Catanaugh. The two wandered as they pleased through the town, and Nautauquaus, seeing Rolfe arrive in his boat from his plantation Varina, where he had built a house for Pocahontas, stepped forward to greet him. His love for Pocahontas made him desire to know her future husband better. Though this man was of another world than his, though his thoughts and ways were different, he was a man as he was; therefore the Indian brave tried to appraise him by the same methods he used in judging the men of his own race—and he was satisfied. Rolfe, recognizing him, shook hands heartily and talked for a while, enquiring about those of his family he had known while a hostage at Werowocomoco.

After Rolfe had left him to enter the Governor's house, Nautauquas turned to find out what Catanaugh was doing, but could see nothing of him.

Catanaugh had not felt the same interest in Rolfe as did his brother and had strolled away towards Pocahontas's house. He had a question he was eager to put to her while Nautauquas was not by. He found his sister in her white gown, with brightly embroidered moccasins on her feet and a circlet of beads and feathers about her head.

"Wilt thou not adorn thyself," he asked, "with the bright chains of the white men?"

"Nay, Brother," she answered; "it may be that I shall wear the strange robes some day, and the bright chains and jewels I will don to-morrow when I am the squaw of an Englishman; but to-day I am still only the daughter of Powhatan."

Catanaugh said nothing further, yet he still stood in the doorway.

"Enter," invited Pocahontas, "and behold how I live."

"I see enough," he answered, turning his head from side to side; "but where dwelleth the white man's Okee?"

"The God of the Christians?" she asked, puzzled at his question; "in the sky above."

"But where do the shamans call to him?" he continued.

"Yonder in the church, that building with the peak to it," she pointed out.

"I will walk some more," announced Catanaugh and left her. When he thought Pocahontas was no longer observing him, he hastened in the direction of the church. During his former short stay in Jamestown he had never been inside and had thought of it—if he paid any attention to it at all—as some kind of a storehouse.

He found the door open and entered quietly, glancing cautiously about until he had assured himself that it was empty. Then he pushed the door to and fastened it with the bolt. This done, he set about examining the building curiously. At the end, towards the rising sun, was an elevation of three steps which made him think of the raised dais that ran across the end of

Powhatan's ceremonial lodge. This was lined with the reddish wood of the cedar, and there was a dark wooden table covered with a white cloth standing in it, and the sun shining through the windows above made the vases filled with flowers glisten brightly. In the part where he stood there were many benches and chairs, and everywhere that it was possible to stand or hang them, was a profusion of fragrant flowering branches.

The very simplicity of the church awed him; had there been a multiplicity of furnishings, of strange objects whose use he could not comprehend, he would have felt he had something definite to watch and fear. His impulse was to flee out into the sunshine, and he turned towards the door. Then he remembered his object in coming and stood still again.

He listened intently, but there was no sound; then taking from the pouch that hung at his side a lump of deer's suet, he smeared it about the sides of the benches and the backs of the chairs. Then with a handful of tobacco taken from the same receptacle he began to sprinkle a small circle in the centre aisle. When this was complete he seated himself crosslegged inside of it. Slowly and deliberately he drew from the larger pouch slung at his back and covered by his long mantle, a mask, somewhat out of shape from its confinement in a small space, and a rattle made of a gourd filled with pebbles. He attached the mask to his face as carefully as if he were to be observed by all his tribe, and laid the rattle across his knees. All these preparations had taken place so quietly that no one who might have been in the church could have discovered the Indian's presence by the aid of his ears alone.

Catanaugh had not come to Jamestown with the sole idea of witnessing his sister's wedding. It was not altogether of his own will that he was now about to undertake a dangerous experiment. He was by no manner of means a coward: his long row of scalps attested to his prowess as a brave; but, unlike Nautauquas, he was one who followed where others led, who obeyed when others commanded. He was fierce in fight, relentless to an enemy, could not even dream as did his father and brother that the white men might become valuable allies and friends. He would gladly have killed them all, and he had grown more and more unwilling that Pocahontas should unite herself to one of these interlopers, as he called them, because he realized that her marriage would make a bond of peace between the two peoples. He had hoped to discover that Pocahontas was being forced into this marriage, in which case he had been prepared to carry her off by some desperate deed at the last moment; but he could not help seeing that she was happy and free in her choice, and would never follow him willingly or go quietly if he tried to make her.

Catanaugh was a member of the secret society of Mediwiwin and he was one who had great faith in medicine men and shamans. He never undertook even a hunting expedition unless he had had a shaman consult his Okee to decide if the day would be a lucky one. In every religious ceremony he would take an active part, would fast if the shamans said it was pleasing to Okee, would kill his enemies or save them for slaves, whichever the shamans suggested. He was himself little of a talker except when after victory he was loud and long in his boasting; but he loved nothing better than to listen when the shamans told tales, as they sat on winter evenings around a lodge fire, or as they lay during the long summer twilights on the soft dried grass, of the transformations of human beings into otter, bear or deer forms, of the pursuit of evil demons, of magic incantations. And the shamans, sure always of an audience in Catanaugh, made much of him, and in many ways without his knowing it, used him as a tool.

Now, it was at their bidding that he sat there motionless, except for his lips, which recited in a tone as regular and as loud as a tree-toad's the words of an incantation they had taught him. And all the time he, who had never trembled before an enemy, was trembling from fear of the unknown. Of course, it was wise for the shamans to make this trial, but he wished it had been possible for one of them to have taken his place. But they knew they would never have got the chance to slip unnoticed as he had done into the lodge of the white man's Okee.

He wondered how this strange Okee would answer his call, for answer he knew he must. The incantation was such strong medicine that no spirit could resist it, especially when he shook the rattle as he did now, rising to his feet and lifting his foot higher and higher, as bending over, he went round and round on his tiptoes, always within the confines of the tobacco circle. The shamans had been determined to find out what kind of an Okee protected the white men, and it was only in this spot they could do so. The palefaces knew so many things the Indian had never learned and which he must learn if he was to hold his own against the terrible medicine of the strangers.

Catanaugh was afraid he might forget some of the magic words the Okee would speak, which the shamans had told him he must hold fast in his mind as he would hold a slippery eel in his hand. Even if he didn't understand them he must just remember them, because they would be wise enough to interpret them. He meant, too, if he only had the courage, to try to make the Okee prevent the wedding.

He had been shaking the rattle gently for fear it might be heard outside the church; but now, anxious to bring this dreadful task to an end, he began to shake it with all his might in one last challenge to the strange spirit.

Bim! Bam! Boum! BOUM! Bim!

Catanaugh jumped like a deer that hears the crackle of a twig behind it. Here in the deep brazen voice of the marriage bells ringing out in the belfry above him he thought he heard the answer his incantation had forced from the white man's Okee. But the voice was so terrible, so loud, that, forgetting the shaman's injunctions, forgetting everything but his need to escape, he rushed to the door, unbolted it frantically and ran, still pursued by the "him, barn, boum" till he reached the fort, where the frightened sentries, who had no orders to keep any Indian from *leaving* the town, let the masked figure through the gates.

Dr. James Buck, who with Dr. Whitaker, was to perform the ceremony, arrived at the church just as the wedding party was starting from the other end of the town. His foot hit against something. He stooped and picked up a rattle and his fingers were covered with brown dust. Hastily seizing a broom which stood in the vestry-room, he swept the tobacco down the aisle and into a corner. The curious rattle he hid with the replaced broom, to be investigated later. Then he took his stand in the chancel, where Dr. Whitaker soon joined him, and through the open door the two clergymen watched their flock approach. Most of them were men, cavaliers as finely dressed, if their garments were somewhat faded, as though they were to sit in Westminster Abbey; soldiers in leathern jerkins; bakers, masons, carpenters, with freshly washed face and hands, in their Sunday garments of fustian and minus workaday aprons; and the few women were in figured tabbies and damasks.

Now when the congregation had filled every seat and were lined up against the walls, a number of Indians, all relatives of Pocahontas, slipped in and stood silently with faces that seemed not alive except for the keenness of their curious eyes. Them through the doorway came Pocahontas and old Opechisco and Nautauquas.

A sudden feeling of the wonder of this marriage overcame Alexander Whitaker. This Indian maiden who was a creature of the woods, shy and proud as a wild animal, was to be married by him to an Englishman with centuries of civilization behind him. What boded it for them both and for their races?

Then with love for the maiden whom he had baptized and with faith in his heart, he listened while Dr. Buck began, until he himself asked in a loud, clear voice:

"Rebecca, wilt thou take this man to be thy wedded husband?"

After the feast was over the bride said to her husband, using his Christian name shyly for the first time:

"John, wilt thou walk with me into the forest a little?"

And Rolfe, nothing loath to escape the noisy crowd, rose to go with her.

"Why dost thou care to come here?" he asked when they found themselves beyond the causeway in the woods flecked with the white of the innumerable dogwood trees.

"Because I feel Jamestown too small to-day, John; because I have ever sought the forest when I was happy or sad; because it seemeth to me that the trees and beasts would be hurt if I did not let them see me this great day."

"'Tis a pretty fancy, but a pagan one, my child," said Rolfe, frowning slightly.

But Pocahontas did not notice. She had caught a glimpse across the leafy branches of the spotted sides of a deer, and she saw a striped chipmunk peer at her from overhead.

"Hey! little friends," she called out gaily to them, "here's Pocahontas come to greet ye. Wish her happiness, that her nest may be filled with nuts. Little Dancer, and cool shade, Bright Eyes, in hot noondays." Then as two wood pigeons flew by she clapped her hands gently together and cried:

"Here's *my* mate, Swift Wings, wish us happiness."

And John Rolfe, sober Englishman that he was, felt uprise in him a new kinship with all the breathing things of the world, and he wondered whether this Indian maiden he had made his wife did not know more of the secrets of the earth than the wise men of Europe.

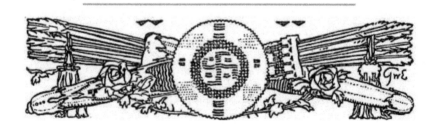

CHAPTER XXI

ON THE TRAIL OF A THIEF

Pocahontas, clothed in European garb, was returning to her home at Varina from the river, whither she had accompanied John Rolfe half a day's journey towards Jamestown. The boatmen had escorted her from the skiff and now doffed their hats as she bade them come no further.

In the two years which had passed since her marriage, the little Indian maiden had learned many things: to speak fluently the language of her husband's people, to wear in public the clothes of his countrywomen, and to use the manners of those of high estate. She had always been accustomed to the deference paid her as the daughter of the great werowance, ruler over thirty tribes, and now she received that of the English, who treated her as the daughter of a powerful ally. For Powhatan had seen the wisdom of keeping peace between Werowocomoco and Jamestown and its settlement up the river of Henrici, of which Rolfe's estate, Varina, was a portion.

Indeed, so stately was the manner of the Lady Rebecca that it was with difficulty that many could recall the wide-eyed maiden who used to come and go at Jamestown.

Now as she ascended the hill her eyes rested upon the home Rolfe had built for her. It was to the eyes of Englishmen, accustomed to the spacious manor houses of their own country, little more than a cabin. But to one who had seen nothing finer than the lodges of her father's towns, it was a very grand structure indeed, with its solid framework of oak, its four rooms, its chimney of brick and its furnishings sent over from London. Her husband had promised her that they should bring back many other wonderful arrangements when they returned from England.

She was a little warm from her climb and was looking forward to the moment when she could discard her clothes for her loose buckskin robe and moccasins. Rolfe, though he did not forbid them altogether, was not pleased at the sight of them; and Pocahontas this day was conscious of a slight feeling of relief that there were to be several days of his absence in which she could forget to be an Englishwoman.

She might forget for a while but only for a while for she was a happy and dutiful wife; but she could never forget that she was a mother, that her wonderful little Thomas, not so white as his father, nor so dark as herself, was waiting for her at the house. She hurried on, thinking of the fun she would have with him: how she would take him down to a stream and let him lie naked on the warm rocks, and how she would sing Indian songs to him and tell him stories of the beasts in the woods, even if he were too little to understand them.

She had left him in his cradle where, protected by its high sides, he was safe for hours at a time, and the workmen who were helping her husband start a tobacco plantation at Varina looked in often to see if he were all right.

She entered the house and hurrying to the cradle, called out:

"Little Rabbit, here I am."

But when she bent over the side, behold! the cradle was empty.

She looked in every room, but found no sign of him. Then she rushed to the door and called. Three of the men came running, and they told her, speaking one on top of the other, how half an hour after she and their master had left one of them had gone to look at the child and found the cradle empty. Since then they had been searching the place over, but with no success.

It was quite impossible for the child to have got away alone; yet who would take him away? Indians or white folk, there was none in all Virginia who would dare injure the grandchild of Powhatan.

When she had listened to what they had to say, Pocahontas bade them go and continue their search. When she was alone she sat down, not on the carven chair a carpenter had made her in Jamestown, but on the floor, as she had so often sat about the lodge fire when she wished to think hard.

After a long period of absolute silence and motionlessness she rose, took off her hat, gown and shoes and clothed herself in her Indian garments. Now she knelt by the cradle and examined the floor carefully, then the sill of the door and the ground in front of it. Something she must have discovered, for she sniffed the air eagerly like a hound that had found the scent. She weighed her decision a moment—should she turn in the direction of Powhata, where she knew Powhatan was staying, or should it be in the direction of Werowocomoco? She turned towards the latter, and stooping every few minutes to examine the ground, proceeded quickly on her quest.

It was the slightest imprint here and there on the earth of a moccasined foot which was the clue. Her brothers and sisters came to see her occasionally; but what purpose could one of them have in stealing her child? No hostile Indians any longer, thanks to the fear Powhatan's might and the English guns had spread among them, were ever seen in this part of the country; so while she hurried on she wondered whence this Indian kidnapper could have come. That it was an Indian she was certain, and that he bore the child she knew, because lying on a rock in the trail she had found a piece of the chain of chinquapins she had amused herself stringing together to place about little Thomas's neck.

Now that she was on the right trail it did not enter her mind to return to her husband's men for help or to send a messenger to Jamestown to fetch him back. She knew well that she was far better fitted than any white man to follow swiftly and surely the way her child had gone. It might be, since the thief had several hours' advantage, that it would be days before she could catch up with him; but if it took years and she had to journey to the end of the world she would not falter nor turn back for help.

As she travelled through the forest in the quick step that was almost a trot, the polish of her English life fell away from her as the leaves fell from the trees above her. She forgot the happenings of the two years since she had been the "Lady Rebecca," forgot her husband; and her baby was no longer the heir of the Rolfes about to be taken across the sea to be shown to his kinsmen; he was her papoose, and as she ran she called out to him all the pet names the Indian mothers loved. When she thought that he might be crying with terror or hunger she began to pray, prayers that came from the depth of her heart that she might reach him before he really suffered. But these prayers were not to the God of the Christians, but to the Okee her fathers had worshipped.

Many times the trail was almost invisible. There was little passing of feet this way and in no place was there anything like a path. But Pocahontas's eyes, keener than even in the days when they had rivalled her brother's in following in play the trail the pursued did his best to cover up, were never long at fault. The ground, the bushes from which raindrops had been shaken, a broken twig—all helped her read the way she was to go. If she could only tell whether she were gaining!

What she would do when she came face to face with the thief she did not know. If he were a strong man who defied her command to give up the grandson of Powhatan, how should she compel him? She had started off so hastily that she had not armed herself with any weapon. But she did not doubt that in some way or other she would wrest her child from him.

The sun was sinking; its beams, she saw, struck now the lower part of the tree trunks. Seeing this, she quickened her step; once the night fell she would have to lie down and wait for morning for fear of missing the trail.

It was almost dark when she reached a sort of open space the size of three lodges width, where doubtless the coming of many wild beasts to drink of a spring that bubbled up in the centre had worn down the growth of young trees. On one side of the ground where moss and creeping crowfoot grew, there were overhanging rocks which formed a small cave not much deeper than a man's height.

No longer could she see a footprint in the dusk, so Pocahontas sadly prepared to spend the night in this shelter. She leaned down and drank long from the spring, and taking off her moccasins, bathed her tired feet in it. Then because she wanted a fire more for its companionship than for the warmth, she gathered twigs, and twirling one in a bit of rotten wood, soon produced a spark that lighted a cheerful blaze.

There was nothing to be gained by staying awake. There was no one from whom she had anything to fear except possibly the thief, and the sooner they met the better pleased she would be. She was drowsy from the warmth of the fire and tired from the long pursuit, so Pocahontas lay down at the entrance of the cave, half within and half without, and in a moment was fast asleep.

Several times during the night she was half awakened by the sound of some young animal crying—perhaps a bear cub, she thought sleepily, but even were the mother bear nearby she had no fear of her.

Later on she dreamed that the mother bear had come into the cave and was sniffing her all over. She opened her eyes and saw the glow from the embers reflected in a pair of eyes above her.

"Go away, old Furry One!" she commanded drowsily. "I'm not afraid of thee. Be off and let me sleep."

But the sound of her own voice wakened her and she raised herself to a sitting position to see whether the bear were obeying her. Against the almost extinguished embers she saw the dim outlines—not of the beast she expected, but of a human being! She sprang up, seized hold of it with her right hand before the other had time to escape, and with her left hand caught up some dried twigs and threw them on the remains of the fire. The wood already heated, ignited at once; the blaze lighted up the little forest room and Pocahontas beheld—Wansutis!

"Where is my child?" cried Pocahontas. "What hast thou done with him? And so it was thou who alone in all the world didst dare steal him from me. What hast thou done with my son? Speak!"

The old woman did not struggle under the firm grasp of the young strong hands. She stood still as if alone, staring into the flames that reddened the circle of trees as if they had been stained with blood.

"What hast thou done with my son?" cried Pocahontas again.

"What hast thou done with *my* son?" asked the old woman, without turning her head to look at Pocahontas.

"Thy son! Claw-of-the-Eagle? Why! I sent thee word many moons ago, Wansutis, that he was dead."

"Hadst thou loved him he had not died."

"I loved him as a sister, Wansutis; my fate lay not in my hands. But Claw-of-the-Eagle is dead, and we mourn him, thou and I"—here she loosened her grasp on the old woman's shoulder, "but my son is alive unless—"

Here a dreadful possibility made her shake like an aspen.

"What hast thou done with my son, Wansutis? What didst thou want with him?"

Wansutis, who was now crouched down looking at the heart of the fire, began to chant as if alone:

"Wansutis's son died in battle. No stronger, fiercer brave was there in all the thirty tribes, and Wansutis's lodge was empty and there was none to hunt for her, to slay deer that she might feed upon fresh meat. Then Wansutis saw a prisoner with strong body, though it was yet small, and Wansutis had a new son, a swift hunter, whose face was ruddy by the firelight, whose presence in her lodge made Wansutis's slumbers quiet. And this son wanted a maiden for his squaw and went forth to play upon his pipes before her. But the maiden would not listen and the river and the maiden killed the brave son of Wansutis, and again her lodge was lonely."

She ceased for a moment, then as if she were reading the words in the flames, she sang more slowly:

"I am old, saith old Wansutis, yet I'll live for many harvests. I will seek another son now; I will bring him to my wigwam. He shall watch me and protect me; he will cheer me in the winters."

Pocahontas interrupted her:

"That then is the reason thou didst steal my child. Thou shalt not keep him; he is not for thy lodge. He goeth with his father and with me to be brought up in the houses of the English."

There came a cry from the forest, the same cry she had heard in her dreams. Without an instant's doubt, Pocahontas sprang into the blackness and in a few moments came back with the baby in her arms. She squatted down by the fire, and felt it over feverishly until she had convinced herself that it was unharmed.

Wansutis now rose.

"Farewell, Princess," she said. "Wansutis will now be returning to her lodge."

Now that she had her child safe again, Pocahontas's kind heart began to speak:

"Wansutis, thou knowest I cannot let thee have my son; but if thou wilt I will pray my father to give thee the next young brave he captures that thou mayst no longer be lonely."

"I will seek no more sons," answered the old woman; "perchance he might set off for a far land and leave me even as thy father's daughter leaveth him."

"But I will return to him," protested Pocahontas.

"Dost thou know that?" the old woman asked, leaning down and peering directly into Pocahontas's face. Her gaze was so full of hatred that Pocahontas drew back in terror.

"I see a ship"—Wansutis began to chant again—"a ship that sails for many days towards the rising sun; but I never see a ship that sails to the sunset. I see a deer from the free forests and it is fettered and its neck is hung with wampum and flowers; but the deer seeks in vain to escape to its bed of ferns in the woodland. I see a bird that is caught where the lodges are closer together than the pebbles on the seashore; but I never see the bird fly free above their lodge tops. I hear the crying of an orphan child; but the mother lieth where she cannot still it."

Pocahontas gazed in horrible fascination at the old woman who, with another harsh laugh, vanished into the darkness.

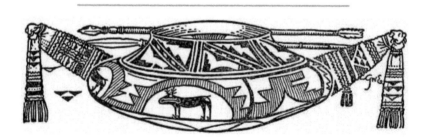

CHAPTER XXII

POCAHONTAS IN ENGLAND

It was an eager, happy Pocahontas that set sail with her husband. Master Rolfe, her child and last—but not in his own estimation—Sir Thomas Dale. With them, too, went Uttamatomakkin, a chief whom Powhatan sent expressly to observe the English and their ways in their own land.

Everything interested Pocahontas on the voyage: the ship herself, the hoisting and furling of sails in calms and tempests, the chanteys of the sailors as they worked, the sight of spouting whales and, as they neared the English coast, the magnificence of a large ship-of-war, a veteran, so declared the captain, of the fleet which went so bravely forth to meet the Spanish Armada. During the long evenings on deck Rolfe told her stories of real deeds of English history and fancied romances of poets; and all were equally wonderful to her.

She could scarcely believe after she had sailed so many weeks over the unchanging ocean, where there were not even the signs to go by that she could read in the trackless forest, that there was land again beyond all the water. It was a marvel which no amount of explanations could simplify that men should be able to guide ships back and forth across this waste. Perhaps this more than any of the wonders she was to see later was what made her esteem the white men's genius most.

And then one day a grey cloud rested on the eastern horizon. Pocahontas saw a new look in her husband's face as he caught sight of it.

"England!" he cried, and then he lifted little Thomas to his shoulder and bade him, "Look at thy father's England."

Even before they stepped ashore at Plymouth Pocahontas's impressions of the country began. On board the ship came officers from the Virginia Company to greet her and put themselves and the exchequer of the Company at her disposal. Was she not the daughter of their Indian ally, a monarch of whose kingdom and power they possessed but the most confused idea. They had arranged, they said, suitable lodgings for Lady Rebecca, Master Rolfe and their infant in London and—with much waving of plumed hats and bowing—they would attend in every manner to her comfort and amusement.

These men were different from any Pocahontas had ever seen; the colonists were all, willy nilly, workers, or at least adventure lovers. These comfortable citizens were of a type as new to her as she to them.

As they rode slowly on their way to London at every mile of the road she cried out with delighted interest and questioned Rolfe without ceasing about the timbered and stuccoed cottages, the beautiful hedges, the rich farms and paddocks filled with horses and cattle. At midday and at night when they stopped at the inns, she was eager to examine everything, from the still-room to the fragrant attics where bunches of herbs hung from the rafters. Yet even in her girlish eagerness she bore herself with a dignity that never allowed the simplest to doubt that, in spite of her dark skin, she was a lady of high birth.

"Ah! John," she said, "this is so fair a land; I know not how thou couldst leave it. I can scarcely wait when I lie abed at night for the morn to come. There is ever something new, and new things, thou knowest, have ever been delightful to my spirit."

"And to mine also, Rebecca," he answered; "for that reason did I seek Wingandacoa and rejoiced in its strangeness, even as thou dost rejoice in the strangeness of my country."

The nearer they drew to London the more there was to see. The highway was filled with those coming and going from town; merchants, farmers with their wares, butchers, travelling artisans, tinkers, peddlers, gypsies, great ladies on horseback or in coaches, who stared at Pocahontas, and gentlemen who questioned the servants about her. And Pocahontas asked Rolfe about all of them, of their condition, their manner of living and what their homes were like within.

When they reached the outskirts of London the crowds increased so that Pocahontas turned to Rolfe and asked:

"Why do all the folk run hither and thither? Is there news of the return of a war party or will they celebrate some great festival?" And she could hardly believe that it was only a gathering such as was to be seen every day. However, as soon as those in the crowd caught sight of her they began to press more closely to gaze at her and at Uttamatomakkin, who looked down at them as unconcernedly as if he had been accustomed to such a sight all his life. Officers of the Virginia Company appeared just then with a coach, into which they conducted Pocahontas, Rolfe and little Thomas, so that they escaped from the curiosity of the crowd.

The days that followed were filled with strange and new enjoyments. Mantuamakers and milliners brought their wares, and Lady Rebecca soon began to distinguish what was best in what they had to offer. She drove in the parks, was rowed down the river in gorgeous barges, had her portrait painted in a gold-trimmed red robe with white collar and cuffs and a hat with a gold band upon it, received the great ladies who came out of curiosity to see for themselves what an Indian princess might be like. All of them had only kind things to say about "the gentle Lady Rebecca."

The Bishop of London was in especial interested in this heathen noblewoman who had become a Christian. He was her escort on many occasions and decided to give a great ball in her honour.

"What will they do, Master Bishop?" she asked of the dignitary who had grown as fond of this new lamb in his flock as if she were his own daughter. "What will all the ladies do at a ball?"

"They will dance."

"Dance!" exclaimed Pocahontas in amazement, who had never seen any other kind of dancing than that which she herself, clad in scant garments, had been wont to practice before she became the wife of an Englishman. This, she now knew, was not of a character suited for English ladies. So, some days later, watching the stately measures and the low reverences of ladies and their cavaliers, Pocahontas wondered what pleasure they could find in such an amusement.

"Perchance, though," she suggested to the good Bishop, "it is some religious ceremony which I know not."

The Bishop laughed so at this idea that Pocahontas could not help laughing, too, though she did not understand what was funny in her speech.

After the dance was over the ladies came to be presented to Lady Rebecca. They did not know what they ought to talk to the stranger about; but one of them in a dull mouse-colored tabby, with sad-colored ribbons, remarked languidly:

"What a fine day we are having."

"Fine!" exclaimed Pocahontas, looking up at the grey sky through the window, which to be sure had not dropped any rain for twenty-four hours, "but the sun is not shining. I should think here in England ye would wear your gayest garments to brighten up the landscape."

"Then the Lady Rebecca doth not like our country?" queried the dame in grey.

"Ah, but yea. In truth it pleaseth me mightily, all but the dark skies. And they tell me that is because of the smoke of the city."

Then Pocahontas's eyes caught sight of an older woman whom Rolfe was escorting towards her. There was something about her appearance that was very pleasing. She was a little above medium height, with hair silvered in front and with cheeks as full of color as the roses she carried in her hands. Pocahontas felt at once that here was a woman whom she could love. Her manner was as dignified as that of any lady in the assemblage, but there was a heartiness in her voice and in her glance which made Pocahontas feel at home as she had not before felt in England.

"This is Lady De La Ware, whose husband, thou knowest, Rebecca, was Governor of our Colony," said Rolfe, "and she hath brought these English roses to thee." Then he strolled off, leaving the two women together.

"They are very beautiful, thy flowers," said Pocahontas, smiling at them and at their giver, "and sweeter than the blossoms that grow in my land."

"Yet those are wonderful, too. I have heard of many glorious trees and vines which grow there and I would that I might see them."

"If thou wilt cross the ocean with us when we return, I will show thee many things that would be as strange to thee as thy land is to me. I would take thee to my father, Powhatan, and he would give dances in thine honour that would not be"—and she laughed again at the thought—"like the ball my Lord Bishop giveth me."

Lady De La Ware smiled, too. She had been told something about the Indian customs.

"Perhaps some day thou shalt take me to thy father's court; but now I am come to take thee to that of our Queen. She hath expressed her desire to see thee shortly. A letter which was written her by Captain John Smith about thee hath made her all the more eager to do honour to one who hath ever befriended the English."

"Captain John Smith hath written to the Queen about me?" said Pocahontas, marvelling.

"In truth, and since his words seemed to me worthy of remembrance, I have kept them in my mind." He begins:

"'If ingratitude be a deadly poyson to all honest vertues, I must be guiltie of that crime if I should omit any meanes to be thankfull. So it is that some ten years ago being in Virginia, and taken prisoner by the power of Powhatan, their chief King, I received from this great savage exceeding great courtesy, especially from his son, Nautauquas, the most manliest, comeliest, boldest spirit I ever saw in a savage, and his sister, Pocahontas, the King's most dear and well beloved daughter, being but a child of twelve or thirteen years of age, whose compassionate pitiful heart, of my desperate estate, gave me much cause to respect her—she hazarded the beating out of her own brains to save mine ... the most and least I can do is to tell you this, because none so oft tried it as myself, and the rather being of so great a spirit, however her stature, if she should not be well received, seeing this Kingdom may rightly have a Kingdom by her means—' And much more there was, Lady Rebecca, which I cannot now recall."

Lady De La Ware did not know that Pocahontas believed Smith dead, and Pocahontas, not imagining anything else, thought Smith must have written this letter from Jamestown before he died; and her heart grew warm thinking how, even dying, he had done what he could for her happiness on the mere chance of her going to England. The truth of the matter was that Smith was then at Plymouth, making ready to start on an expedition to New England; and though he did not expect to see Pocahontas, he wished England, and first of all England's Queen, to know what they owed this Indian girl.

It happened not long after that "La Belle Sauvage," as the Londoners sometimes called Pocahontas, and Rolfe were being entertained at a fair country seat. An English girl, much of the age of her guest, whose curiosity about the ways of the Indians was restrained only by her courtesy, had been showing her through the beautiful old garden. They had talked of Virginia, and Mistress Alicia coaxed:

"Wilt thou not take me with thee. Lady Rebecca, when thou returnest thither?

"But see," and she peered through an opening in the high yew hedge, "yonder cometh Master Rolfe with a party of gentlemen. Oh! one of them is a brave figure of a man, though he weareth not such fine clothes as some of the others. By my troth! 'tis Captain John Smith, and of course he cometh to greet thee. I would I might stay to hear what ye two old friends have to say to each other."

It seemed to Pocahontas that hours elapsed during the few minutes she was alone after Mistress Alicia left her, while her husband was guiding her guests to her through the garden's winding mazes. How could Smith be alive when she knew that he was dead? Even as she caught in the distance the sound of his voice, she asked herself if in truth she had ever heard of his death from anyone but the councillors in Jamestown.

The well-known voice was no longer weak as when she had last heard it bid her farewell. There they were, the gentlemen all bowing to her but remaining in the background, while Rolfe came forward with Smith.

"I have brought thee an old friend, Rebecca," he said.

Pocahontas saluted him, but words were impossible.

John Smith afterwards wrote concerning this interview:

"After a modest salutation, without any word, she turned about, obscured her face, as not seeming well contented, and in that humor her husband with divers others, we all left her two or three hours."

Seeing that she preferred to be alone, the men departed to talk over the affairs of the Virginia Colony since Smith had left Jamestown. Pocahontas, sitting quietly on a garden bench near the carp pond, went over in her thought all that had taken place in her own life since then.

Then she saw him coming towards her again, alone, and she stretched out her hand to him.

"My father," she cried, "dost thou remember the old days in Wingandacoa when thou earnest first to Werowocomoco and wert my prisoner?"

"I remember well. Lady Rebecca," he said, leaning down to kiss her hand, "and I am ever thy most grateful debtor."

"Call me not by that strange name. Matoaka am I for thee as always. Dost thou remember when I came at night through the forest to warn thee?"

"I remember, Matoaka; how could I forget it?"

"Dost thou remember the day when, lying wounded before thy door, thou didst make me promise to be ever a friend to Jamestown and the English?"

"I have thought of it many a day."

"I have kept my promise, Father, have I not?"

"Nobly, Matoaka; but it is not meet that thou shouldst call me father."

Then Pocahontas tossed her head emphatically, and this gesture brought back to Smith the bright young Indian maiden who, for a moment, had seemed to him disguised by the stately clothes of an English matron.

"Thou didst promise Powhatan," she cried, "what was thine should be his, and he the like to thee; thou calledst him father, being in his land a stranger, and by the same reason so must I do thee."

"But, Princess," he objected, "it is different here. The King would like it not if I allowed it here; he might say it was indeed truth what mine enemies say of me, that I plan to raise myself above them."

"Wert thou afraid to come into my father's country and caused fear in him and all his people but me, and fearest thou here I should call thee father? I tell thee then I will and thou shalt call me child, and so will I be for ever and ever thy countryman."

Smith smiled at her eagerness, yet was deeply touched by it.

"Call me then what thou wilt; I can fear no evil that might come to me from thee."

Pocahontas then spoke a few words to him in the Powhatan tongue, anxious to see if he still remembered it. And he answered her in her language. She was silent, but Smith could see that something was disturbing her.

"What is it, Matoaka; what words wait to cross the ford of thy lips?" he asked.

"They did tell me always," she replied, "that thou wert dead and I knew no more till I came to Plymouth, yet Powhatan did command Uttamatomakkin to seek thee and know the truth, because thy countrymen will lie much."

"Think of it no more. Little Sister, if thou still let me call thee that. I am not dead yet and I have many journeys to make. I thank fate I had not yet sailed for that coast to the north of Jamestown they call 'New England,' so that I might greet thee once again. When I return we shall have many more talks together."

"I shall not be here, Father; we too shall set sail ere long. I have been happy here in thy land, but I am now suffering from an illness they tell me is called homesickness."

"That is an illness which may be easily remedied, Matoaka. But when thou art come again to Wingandacoa forget not the England and the friends which can never forget thee."

In the days that followed Lady De La Ware, touched by the affection Pocahontas manifested towards her, accompanied her everywhere, to the wonderful masque written by the poet, Ben Jonson, which was performed at the Twelfth Night festival, and to the play written by Master Will Shakespeare that he called "The Tempest," which represented court folk cast ashore on an island in the western ocean.

Everything was so full of interest that her new life seemed to be leading her further and further away from the old simple existence of forest and river. Then came the presentation to the Queen, Anne of Denmark, consort of James First of England and Sixth of Scotland. Lady De La Ware had seen that Lady Rebecca's costume suited her dark skin and hair.

Before coming to the presence chamber there were many halls and anterooms filled with courtiers and ladies, whose curious glances might have dismayed any woman who had not grown accustomed to a life at court; but Pocahontas passed on unconscious of them all.

In the large hall which they entered last, hung with rich tapestries and furnished with dark oaken chairs and settles covered with royal purple velvet, a few pages and the Queen's ladies alone kept her company. As Pocahontas and Lady De La Ware advanced, the Queen motioned every one else to withdraw to the farther end of the chamber. She curtsied in return to the obeisances made by Pocahontas and her sponsor, but did not stretch forth her hand to be kissed as she would have done had she not considered this stranger before her as a princess of royal blood.

"I thank thee for coming," she said graciously. "I have much desired to see thee. Captain Smith was right when he reminded me of what our people owe thee, he most of all."

"He was dear to my people also," answered Pocahontas.

"Hath Your Majesty heard how men speak of Captain Smith in the Colony?" asked Lady De La Ware. "My brother who is still at Jamestown wrote me that one of the colonists regretting the great Captain's departure said of him:

"What shall I say of him but thus we lost him, that in all his proceedings made justice his first guide, and experience his second, ever hating baseness, sloth, pride, and indignity more than any dangers; that never allowed more for himself than his soldiers with him; that upon no danger would send them where he would not lead them himself; that would never see us want what he either had or could get us; that would rather want than borrow, or starve than not pay; that loved action more than words, and hated falsehood and covetousness more than death; whose adventures were our lives, and whose loss our death.'"

"Tell me of thy long voyage," then questioned her majesty; and seating herself, made room for Pocahontas beside her, while Lady De La Ware moved off to talk with one of the ladies. "I do not see how men, and more especially women, dare trust themselves for so long on the sea. When I had been married by proxy to my lord, the King, I tried to go by ship from Denmark to Scotland, but the tempests were so fierce that we had to put in to Norway, scarce saving our lives; and thither came my gracious lord, against the prayers of his councillors who tried to dissuade him from venturing his precious safety in winter storms. Oh! I have no love of the sea."

"I did not fear it," said Pocahontas, "but I thought it would never end. Had I been alone, though, without my husband and my child"—then, not knowing that court etiquette did not sanction the changing the subject of conversation by any one but the sovereign, she asked: "And how many children hast thou?"

Queen Anne was pleased with her naturalness and told her of her son and daughter and of the wonderful Prince Henry whom she had lost.

While they sat talking about their children as quietly as two plain housewives, there was a commotion at the end of the hall. The pages seemed very excited and uncertain what they ought to do. However, they could not have prevented if they would, and into the hall, clad in his long mantle, moccasins and with his headdress of feathers, strode Uttamatomakkin. Pocahontas, looking up, saw that he was examining eagerly all the furnishings of the hall and then his gaze was bent upon the Queen.

"Is yon the squaw of the great white werowance?" he asked, "and is this their ceremonial lodge? I have already beheld the King and he is a weak little creature whom any child at Werowocomoco could knock down."

"Who is he, and what doth he say?" asked the Queen, who was delighted at his strange appearance.

"It is one of my people, Madame, and he wishes to know if thou art indeed the Queen that he may tell of thee when he returneth to Wingandacoa." She did not think it wise to repeat the rest of his remarks.

The Queen, whose curiosity was great in regard to this strange race from overseas of whom she had heard so many tales, beckoned to Uttamatomakkin to come closer. The Indian walked stolidly to the dais where she stood.

"What is this mantle made of?" asked the sovereign, taking up an end of the painted and embroidered deerskin robe and rubbing it critically between her fingers.

Uttamatomakkin, thinking this was the English form of salutation and not intending to be outdone in politeness, caught hold of Queen Anne's velvet skirt, and to the accompaniment of little shrieks of dismay from the ladies-in-waiting, fingered it in the same manner.

"That must thou not do," remonstrated Pocahontas, trying not to laugh; but Uttamatomakkin grunted:

"Why should I not do what a squaw doth?"

The Queen recovered her equanimity and in sign of her good will unfastened a golden brooch and pinned it on the Indian's broad shoulder. Then the chief broke off from his girdle a string of wampum, and before any one realized what he intended doing, he had fastened it to a pearl pin on the Queen's bodice.

"I see I cannot get the better of him. Lady Rebecca," laughed her Majesty; "but ask him what he doth with yon long stick."

The pages, whose interest in this savage overcame for the moment their habit of etiquette, had approached little by little towards the end of the hall where he stood. They watched eagerly and with a certain dread of the unknown while he took from his pouch a white stick and his knife from his girdle. The stick, they saw, was covered with tiny nicks; and the Indian, looking from one person to another, made many more marks on the wand.

"What is it thou dost, Uttamatomakkin?" asked Pocahontas.

"The werowance, thy father, told me to mark and let him know when I return how many white folk there were in this land. I made a cut for each one I counted at first, but my stick is all but covered now and the Powhatan will not know how the palefaces swarm here like bees in a hollow tree."

Pocahontas repeated to the Queen what he had said, and her Majesty was greatly amused.

"But thou dost not plan to return to Virginia for a long; time yet?" she asked.

"Much I like thy land, and its pleasant folk," answered Pocahontas as she rose to go. "But the time draweth near for us to set sail westward again. Farewell."

Then, accompanied by Lady De La Ware and Uttamatomakkin, she left the audience chamber.

"The Lady Rebecca," said the Queen to her ladies when the curtains had fallen behind Pocahontas, "is one of the gentlest ladies England hath ever welcomed."